GUIDANCE:
LIVING THE INSPIRED LIFE

By Robert Perry

Book #4 in a Series of
Commentaries on *A Course in Miracles*®

This is the fourth book in a series, each of which deals with a particular theme from the modern spiritual teaching *A Course in Miracles*. The books assume a familiarity with the Course, yet they might be of some benefit even if you have no acquaintance with the Course. If you would like to receive future books directly from the publisher, or would like to receive the newsletter that accompanies this series, please write us at the address below:

The Circle of Atonement
Teaching and Healing Center
P.O. Box 4238
West Sedona, AZ 86340
(520) 282-0790, Fax (520) 282-0523
http://nen.sedona.net/circleofa/

The references to *A Course in Miracles* in this book are given for both the first and second editions. First are given the volume and page number for the first edition; then comes a semi-colon, followed by notations for the second edition. Each reference begins with a letter, which denotes the particular volume of the Course: T=Text, W= Workbook, M=Manual for Teachers, C=Clarification of Terms, P=Psychotherapy pamphlet, S=Song of Prayer. After this letter comes a series of numbers, which differ from volume to volume:

T, P, or S-chapter.section.paragraph:sentence
W-part (I or II).lesson.paragraph:sentence
M or C-section.paragraph:sentence

The ideas represented herein are the personal interpretation and understanding of the author and are not necessarily endorsed by the copyright holder of *A Course in Miracles*: Foundation for *A Course in Miracles*, 1275 Tennanah Lake Road, Roscoe, NY 12776-5905.

Published by The Circle of Atonement: Teaching and Healing Center
Printed in the United States of America
Reformatted for Third Printing

Cover idea by David Sunfellow; Cover art by Robert Perry, based on a photograph by Bob Sacha.
Typesetting by Karen Reider

CONTENTS

Introduction

A *Course in Miracles* frequently urges us to "ask the Holy Spirit everything, and leave all decisions to His gentle counsel" (Text, p. 257; T-14.III.12:6). The impression created is that there is this Voice in your mind that will, in clear English, answer every question you may pose to It, and, like a combination sports announcer and coach, give you a running interpretation of what is happening in your life and a running advisement on what you should do, where you should go, what you should say and to whom. Nothing beyond tiny hints is really ever said about any problems you may have in getting this guidance. It seems to be assumed that it will simply be there in all circumstances whenever you turn to it.

Yet it is the problems that loom largest for most Course students, and spiritual students in general. The most common thing that I hear is, "I do ask; I just don't get anything." I recently saw the results of a poll which suggested that a large percentage of Americans pray for guidance, but that most feel like they never get answers. In response to the sheer frustration of it all, Course students have adopted many different postures in relation to guidance. Some discount it and suggest that you should just follow your own common sense. Some hope they are getting it whether they are aware of it or not. Some worry endlessly about whether or not they are doing God's Will. And most everyone has an instant anger reaction to those who blithely suggest they are being guided by the Unseen Hand in the sky, yet who seem to be merely granting Divine sanction to their ego's own barely disguised appetites.

I have been wanting to write a book on guidance for years.

For now, it will have to be a booklet, but I hope to write on this topic more fully later on. For about nine years now it has been a cornerstone of my life. I have often remarked that, while I am not the most loving and forgiving person, one thing on the spiritual path that I have learned is how to be guided. Hopefully, my experience will bring hope to some people, for when it comes to hearing an inner voice–the conventional image of being guided--I am stone deaf. I have never heard a thing. Apparently my inner pipes are so clogged that the Holy Spirit has thrown up His hands in despair and has had to turn to other means in order to reach me. Yet, He seems to have little problem with this, for I do feel constantly bathed in His direction.

Up until I was 23 I was the architect of my own life. I made my own decisions and planned my own future. In fact, I had great plans for my future. Then, it seemed like God stepped into my life and just trashed all my plans. At that point it became clear to me, to my absolute astonishment, that He had a very definite plan for me. Suddenly, it appeared as if all the things in my life, things which had seemed to be blown here and there by the random winds of human choice and physical law, got up and began dancing as one to the music of God's plan. It was the strangest experience, and very real; one that has only increased as time has gone on. It has been a source of never-ending fascination and meaning for me. For it has been real experiential proof that an infinitely wise and loving Mind will act upon the chaotic material of this splintered world and bring order out of it; something like the Genesis story, in which God moved over the face of the deep, bringing light and life out of the darkness of the void. In my experience it is as if some Mind is impressing Itself onto the substance of my life, with such strength yet such fluidity that it just does not seem to matter what I think or plan or want. In the end, It will have Its way with me.

Much of my experience of guidance has come from working with a community of people who are dedicated to being guided. In fact, the event I referred to above as God barging into my life was the event of the birth of this community. To a very significant degree our little community has been based on guidance. We have had no human leader but have sincerely sought to make the Spirit's leading the real basis for our decisions, perspectives and sense of purpose. I have benefitted immeasurably from being with people who are seeking guidance and working with it in many of its forms, which include inner voices, dreams, intuitions, outer signs and synchronicities, etc. I have especially learned from working with my friend and spiritual partner, Sandy Fraser, who hears what our community has come to regard as a very helpful inner voice; and who, as a result, will be turning up in these pages repeatedly.

Over time I have realized that guidance is both an art and a science, something that must be grown into. In my first years with it I made many missteps and many enthusiastic but wrong predictions. Over time I have come to see that it is far more subtle and complex than I would have guessed at first. I have learned that it is not about predicting future events, but about choosing to inwardly move with the flow of the Spirit in the present moment. Over time I have learned how to move with that flow a little more gracefully, so that now guidance is a far more reliable process for me than it was in the beginning. Yet still I am just a neophyte. I am in a constant process of learning new things about guidance, a process that I am sure will not end until I am fully awake.

Much of my purpose in writing this booklet is to communicate some of what I have learned about guidance. This is quite different from my normal objective in this booklet series of trying to simply interpret the Course. There will be a great deal of the Course in here and, in fact, I am not quite sure where the Course ends and my personal learnings begin. Yet still my own experience is a major contributor and so the booklet is going to be somewhat limited by my personal temperament and by what I have personally experienced. Since each of us needs to find our own way of being guided, everything in here may not be appropriate for you. If what I say does not sit right inside, then please follow what does.

Guidance is for real. This is perhaps the main thing that I would communicate. It need not be sporadic and it does not fit in with the normal way in which we do things. However problematic it may seem to be, making the Holy Spirit the Author and Architect of our lives is truly possible. It is a viable and comprehensive alternative to the way we have been taught to find our way through the maze of this world. I hope that this booklet will help you along the road to making His guidance a foundation of your life.

CHAPTER 1

Course Theory
on Guidance

Throughout this booklet I will be drawing on the Course and sincerely hope I never contradict the Course. Yet, as I have said, much of the booklet is going to be based on my personal experience of guidance. And so I wanted to start it out with an overview of what exactly the Course itself says on this topic.

Guidance is a relatively minor topic in the Course. In preparation for writing this booklet I collected everything I could find on guidance in the Course, and I came up with about 20 pages— that's all. Compared to such topics as forgiveness or guilt or special relationships, then, guidance is given a fairly small amount of press in the Course. Yet the reason for this, I think, must be understood. It is not because the Course sometimes tells us to seek guidance and sometimes suggests we should decide by ourselves. The reason is that the Course is not primarily concerned with our decisions, with the process of structuring our lives and moving through our world. It is concerned with the content of our thoughts, the substance of our interpretations of ourselves and others. Decision-making, however, is not irrelevant to the Course's path. And whenever the topic of decision-making does come up, the Course always says "let the Holy Spirit decide." It never says, "Ah, what the heck, just make up your own mind."

In fact, I find the Course uncompromising if not a bit extreme on this point. As I said earlier, I and the community of which I am part have become extremely guidance-oriented, feeling a very strong consciousness that our lives are overseen by a plan that is prior to and independent of our ideas and preferences, and believing that in any decision the main thing is to check in with the Spirit behind this plan. Yet, as we look around, we have not found much kinship with other groups and other teachings on this point. We often read about other communities and feel a great deal in common with them, but we only rarely feel commonality on this particular point.

More than any other teaching of which I am aware, the Course reflects this profound orientation toward guidance. Its orientation can be summarized in two simple ideas: 1) The Holy Spirit is the perfect Parental Influence in relation to our earthly lives; and 2) We are complete children in this respect, who have no ability and no business in making our own decisions.

The Perfect Parent

The Course paints a picture of the Holy Spirit that in the end, even though the Course does not use this word, resembles nothing so much as the absolute perfect Parent. The Course makes it very clear that the Holy Spirit is not your Father, your Creator. But it is equally clear that He is here to represent your Father in this world, to play a fatherly role in relation to your passage through time and space. In fact, He is supposed to play an even greater role than any earthly father should play in relation to his children. For much of a father's role is to stand back and let a child unfold from within, to let that seed of maturity within the child simply express itself through the child. Yet, unlike the human father, the Holy Spirit is within. He is the true seed of maturity in every heart. Therefore, the Holy Spirit is here to guide and direct literally everything in your earthly life.

Let us look at the number of things that the Course says He should be allowed to guide for us. First, He is a spiritual Teacher, Who will communicate from within the truth about reality, "About the Love your Father has for you. About the endless joy He offers you" (Workbook, p. 133; W-pI.76.10:4-5), "About salvation and the gift of peace. About the end of sin and guilt and death. About the role forgiveness has in Him" (Song of Prayer, p. 14).

Based on the basic truths that He teaches, His primary role is to guide and heal our thinking (the guidance of behavior and outer situations is strictly secondary). He is here to transform our thinking, to replace our wrong-minded thoughts with right-minded thoughts. And He is here to actually think through us. The Course tells us repeatedly that the ongoing, second-by-second process of interpreting your world and ordering your thoughts should be left up to Him. We are told that "you have no basis at all for ordering your thoughts" (Text, p. 273; T-14.X.6:1), and that "analyzing the motives of others is hazardous to you" (Text, p. 200; T-12.I.1:6). Thus you should "Let Him be Judge...of everything that seems to happen to you in this world" (Workbook, p. 272; W-pI.151.9:6).

His role, however, does not stop with your internal interpretations, but extends to your decisions about your outer life. According to the Course, the teacher of God "does not make his own decisions; he asks his Teacher for His answer, and it is this he follows as his guide for action" (Manual, p. 25; M-9.2:2). And this does not just mean major decisions. The Holy Spirit is supposed to tell us "what to do and where to go; to whom to speak and what to say to him, what thoughts to think, what words to give the world" (Workbook, p.424; W-pII.275.2:1-3). Thus, His guidance should cover the whole gamut of our lives, from our general "life situation" (Manual, p. 25; M-9) to our decisions about how to go through the day (Text, p. 581; T-30.I.2:2), and even the specific words we use (Manual, p. 51; M-21.4:5).

Finally, the Holy Spirit has a plan for our lives. If we allow Him, He will communicate to us our special function (in common parlance, our "life purpose"), will arrange situations to suit that function (Text, p. 404: T-20.IV.8), will bring us the people with whom we are to carry out that function, and will even decide what possessions we are to have and will supply us with them (Text, p. 238-239; T-13.VII.10-13) as well as with the money we need (Psychotherapy, p. 21-22).

As you can see, absolutely everything is to be given over into His care. Literally nothing is outside His province. The more advanced we become the more innocent we will be of our own mental machinations and independent will, and the more we will simply be carried along, floating on our backs on a river of peace. Our thoughts, interpretations, actions and words will simply be the flow of the river welling up through us and out of us. It will be effortless:

> When you have learned how to decide with God, all decisions become as easy and right as breathing. There is no effort, and you will be led as gently as if you were being carried down a quiet path in summer. Only your own volition seems to make deciding hard. The Holy Spirit will not delay in answering your every question what to do. He knows. And He will tell you, and then do it for you. You who are tired will find this is more restful than sleep. For you can bring your guilt into sleeping, but not into this. (Text, p. 260-261; T-14.IV.6)

4

There are two very good reasons that we should relegate to Him such authority. The second one we will get to shortly; the first reason is that He is perfectly suited to this role. To begin with, He possesses literally omniscient awareness about the roads we can choose and the results of each one—its effects not only on ourselves, but on everyone involved.

> There is Someone with you Whose judgment is perfect. He does know all the facts; past, present and to come. He does know all the effects of His judgment on everyone and everything involved in any way. And He is wholly fair to everyone, for there is no distortion in His perception.
>
> (Manual, p. 27; M-10.4:7-10)

Further, He has only boundless love for us. The Course tells us over and over again that He only gives, and gives us everything. "He will never ask what you have done to make you worthy of the gift of God....for He knows that you are worthy of everything God wills for you" (Text, p. 257; T-14.III.11:4,6). He tells us everything we need to know, holding nothing back: "He will not withhold all answers that you need for anything that seems to trouble you" (Workbook, p. 477; W-pII-epilogue.1:6). He does not make things hard for us; does not give us "disaster...to be perceived as 'good' some day but now in form of pain" (Text, p. 520; T-26.VIII.7:9). Any delay or difficulty or limitation in getting guidance comes solely from the network of resistance in our own minds, never from Him.

The Holy Spirit has our best interests in mind. This is a great blessing, since, according to the Course, we do not. Thus, against our attraction to guilt and pain, "the Holy Spirit is [our] only Friend" (Text, p. 258; T-14.III.13:5). Therefore, letting Him guide us is the surest road to pure happiness. It is a road that will prove itself worthy by its results: "You have very little trust in me as yet, but it will increase as you turn more and more often to me instead of to your ego for guidance. The results will convince you increasingly that this choice is the only sane one you can make" (Text, p.61; T-4.VI.3:1-2).

He will adapt Himself fully to our individual needs. "There is...no set pattern, since training is always highly individualized" (Manual, p. 25; M-9.1:5). Further, He carries only the deepest respect for our own process of choice. Thus, unlike many Judaeo-Christian images, He never forces Himself on us and can serenely and patiently wait a thousand years as easily as a second.

> The Voice of the Holy Spirit does not command, because it is incapable of arrogance. It does not demand, because it does not seek control. It does not overcome, because it does not attack. It merely reminds. It is compelling only because of what it reminds you of.   (Text, p. 70; T-5.II.7:1-5)

In summary, the Holy Spirit is absolutely trustworthy in the role of Guide for our lives. We can place ourselves in His hands with the same unself-conscious trust with which a child places her hand in her father's.

A dependent child

The second reason that we should give our lives over into the care of the Holy Spirit is that we are simply incapable of thinking, speaking or acting effectively on our own. This is not a popular idea, but in light of the Course's high standards for appropriate thought and behavior, it does not take much reflection to see its truth.

> In order to judge anything rightly, one would have to be fully aware of an inconceivably wide range of things; past, present and to come. One would have to recognize in advance all the effects of his judgments on everyone and everything involved in them in any way. And one would have to be certain there is no distortion in his perception, so that his judgment would

be wholly fair to everyone on whom it rests now and in the future. Who is in a position to do this? Who except in grandiose fantasies would claim this for himself?

(Manual, p. 26; M-10.3:3-7)

Such a function presupposes a knowledge that no one here can have; a certainty of past, present and future, and of all the effects that may occur in them. Only from this omniscient point of view would such a role be possible. Yet no perception is omniscient, nor is the tiny self of one alone against the universe able to assume he has such wisdom except in madness.

(Psychotherapy, p. 15)

Further, there is a deeper reason for our not deciding, besides our inadequacy in knowledge and intelligence. Deciding by ourselves assumes that we are by ourselves, that we are limited, discrete beings. Yet the thought that you are just this "you" and nothing more, that you are just "a little, broken bit..." and not "the whole picture" (Text, p. 557; T-28.IV.8:3), is the root error. It is an attack on the true grandeur of your Self. Thus, a recurring theme in the Course's discussions of guidance is that if we decide by ourselves we will only reproduce the fundamental decision that put us by ourselves in the first place.

Before you make any decisions for yourself, remember that you have decided against your function in Heaven, and then consider carefully whether you want to make decisions here.

(Text, p. 260; T-14.IV.5:1)

We are told that taking the function of decision-making to ourselves reflects the original basis of guilt and fear—our primordial attempt to usurp God's Function (Manual, p. 67; M-29.3:6). And that deciding by ourselves will simply reproduce our basic (unconscious) decision that salvation lies in collecting guilt (Text, p. 257-258; T-14.III.13:3-4). We are also told it will express our attraction to pain, since in our deciding we will try to protect the self we think we are, a "self" which is an attack on our real

Self. Thus, "Without His guidance you...will decide against your peace as surely as you decided that salvation lay in you alone" (Text, p. 258: T-14.III.14:4).

The Course, therefore, is absolutely emphatic that we must resign as our own guide. This is one of its cardinal themes. This is meant first on a very abstract level, that we must cease to think that we can successfully figure out the nature of reality—the true identity of ourselves and others and the true meaning of the things we behold in the world. But resigning as our own guide is also meant very specifically. It means that we must lay aside the constant process of deciding what we need, what will make us happy. "Your function here is only to decide against deciding what you want, in recognition that you do not know. How, then, can you decide what you should do?" (Text, p. 260; T-14.IV.5:2-3). We can get a grasp of just how specifically the Course means this when it tells us that we are completely unable to decide what physical possessions we need. "Therefore ask not of yourself what [physical things] you need, for you do not know, and your advice to yourself will hurt you" (Text, p. 239; T-13.VII.11:5).

Think about this. The implication here is that our decisions about what situations, spouses, friends, jobs, television shows, clothes, meals, houses, vacations, cars, etc., we want in our lives will hurt us. We simply do not have a fraction of the information and intelligence we would need to decide such things. And, as if that were not enough, we are attracted to what hurts us. The "self" that we are trying to feed, protect, comfort and fulfill is an attack on who we really are.

So we must, then, let the Holy Spirit "be the only Guide that you would follow to salvation" (Text, p. 258; T-14.III.14:1). And, even once we seek to follow Him, this disparity between our role and His continues. This means that whenever guidance is delayed, does not come, or causes painful results, the problem is

8

always on our end. "...this does not mean that the guide is untrustworthy. In this case, it always means that the follower is" (Text, p. 125; T-7.X.5:8-9). As far as I can discern from the Course, there are three causes in us that block, limit or distort our reception of guidance:

1. Our belief that we can do it on our own. "It is only because you think that you can run some little part, or deal with certain aspects of your life alone, that the guidance of the Holy Spirit is limited" (Text, p. 277; T-14.XI.8:4).

2. Our fear of the Holy Spirit. We often recoil from His guidance "for fear of what you think it will demand of you" (Text, p. 197; T-11.VIII.5:7), and for fear that it will force itself upon us. Our minds are closed; we are unwilling to hear.

3. Our withdrawal from true relationship with others. This is a surprising one, but it is mentioned several times in the Course. We are told twice that we must see the Holy Spirit in our brother if we would strengthen His Voice in ourselves (Text, p. 72; T-5.III.4 and Text, p. 153; T-9.II.6). We are also told the Holy Spirit's blessings to us are delayed in time to the extent we wish our brother to be separated from us in space (Text, p. 519-520; T-26.VIII).

The idea that we are mere children that need the support and guidance of a Parent is a distasteful one for many of us. And not only so to worldly values centered on independence and self-reliance. Many spiritual teachings would also look askance at this idea from the Course. Some New Age teachings, for instance, see this kind of reliance on the Spirit as an immature phase that must be outgrown if we would take our real role as creator of our (illusory) reality. This point—that a parent/child relationship with the Holy Spirit is one that degrades or belittles us—is an important one and needs to be addressed.

In reality, says the Course, we are the adult Christ, the single Self that God created as His one Son. Our apparent identity of being a separate mind with limited powers that lives in a physical body and is surrounded by an outer "reality," is a product of the ego. It has nothing to do with our true Self, Which is bodiless, limitless and has nothing outside of It. Thus, even though my Self is within me, It is completely outside of the whole framework of this tiny personality in this minuscule body.

Since this framework of separate-mind-living-in-a-body is egoic, if we use that framework to run our lives we will be expressing ego. And we will be shutting out our true Self. To decide by ourselves, as I implied earlier, is to reinforce the basic condition of being by ourselves, and thus being alienated from our Self.

The Course's path to finding our Self, then, is not to invest more authority and sufficiency in the separate mind, but rather to undermine its authority and sufficiency. We must humble the framework of separated identity. We must realize that of ourselves we know nothing, have no power, do not know what we want and cannot guide ourselves. We must realize, as the Course reminds us many times, that of ourselves we are nothing. Given the limitations we have laid on ourselves, the most honest thing we can do is to acknowledge that in our current condition we are little children. For, "Little children recognize that they do not understand what they perceive..." (Text, p. 196; T-11.VIII.2:2).

This, however, is extremely different from traditional Christian humility. There we humble ourselves because we truly are lowly, weak and sinful. In the Course, however, we humble our separated minds because they are a block to the realization of the magnitude and grandeur of Who we really are. "Let me not forget myself is nothing, but my Self is all" (Workbook, p. 473; W-pII.358.1:7). In other words, we must take power, reality and identity away from our separated minds and transfer them to our Christ Mind.

This is where the Holy Spirit comes in. Because you are so out of touch with your Christ Self, the Holy Spirit, in a sense, plays that Self for you. He steps in as an inner "Teacher...Who represents the other Self in you" (Workbook, p. 210; W-pI.121.6:2). By turning over power to Him, you learn to relate to your true Self as It actually is. For, like your Self, the Holy Spirit is within you, but He is most definitely outside the tiny powers and faculties wielded by your conscious mind.

This, I believe, is similar to what is said about relationship with a guru. For the guru, in a sense, plays your true Self for you, a role you are as yet incompetent to fill. The difference in the Course's view is that the Holy Spirit is not another person who still has an ego and seems to be outside of you. Outer gurus can easily be disempowering. Yet the Holy Spirit is an inner Guru. In fact, even though the Course approves of the idea of teachers who in some sense take on students, it sees even the most advanced teachers as fellow disciples of the real Guru, the Holy Spirit.

The result of bowing to the Spirit's Authority within you is that your separated mind gets out of the way, allowing your sense of identity to be drawn upward and expanded. Your sense of self moves away from your current body-mind and toward your real Self. As this happens, power starts to flow through your body-mind, yet it is power that originates Somewhere else and thus draws you to Its Source. You ultimately relinquish your current sense of self and all its limitations, and finally re-identify with what is beyond even the Holy Spirit, with your true and immortal Self.

In other words, admitting that you are currently a child and letting the Holy Spirit take the reigns is not disempowering. It is an authentic way to reclaim your true inheritance, your forgotten power.

Here again is the paradox often referred to in the course. To say, "Of myself I can do nothing" is to gain all power. And yet it is but a seeming paradox. As God created you, you have all power. The image you made of yourself has none. The Holy Spirit knows the truth about you....To ask the Holy Spirit to decide for you is simply to accept your true inheritance. (Manual, p. 67-68; M-29.4:1-6,5:4)

CHAPTER 2

The Place of Guidance on the Spiritual Path

Before we talk about actually receiving and working with guidance, it seems important to get clear on the place that guidance has on the spiritual path, its legitimate place and the benefits involved in being guided, as well as misconceptions about guidance and over-evaluations of its true role.

The ego's use of guidance

The most common ego response to guidance is simply to avoid it, or at least to limit it to certain "safe" parts of our lives. Yet, if you insist on turning to the Holy Spirit for guidance, the ego can accommodate this quite nicely. What it does is distort the purpose of guidance and thereby fit guidance into its framework, its approach to life. This is a neat trick, since the whole purpose of guidance is to, in the end, completely disintegrate the ego's framework.

The ego's approach to life is heavily form-oriented. All it cares about are physical objects and physical events. Its whole goal is to have the outer world treat it "right," to have people's words and opinions, as well as the objects, money and physical conditions around it, all "say" to it what it wants to hear. It wants the outer world to bestow on it approval, protection and reality.

Now, when we "get spiritual," this form-orientation, of course, remains pretty intact. Thus, when we turn to guidance, our natural hope is that now, not I, but the Holy Spirit is going to make things go my way, that He is going to control my world so that it protects and affirms my ego. This usually includes the hope that He is going to lavish the world's approval on my ego better than I ever could.

And there is another thing that happens when we "get spiritual," a thing which is often in conflict with the above impulse. This is that we become intensely concerned with the "right" forms, the "spiritual" forms: the "right" foods, clothing, jobs and, perhaps even more important, the right direction for our lives. This, of course, often includes going without forms, sacrificing outer things for the sake of being holy. For, whereas in the blatant ego mode we wanted outer events to shine approval on our ego to prove how important it is, now we have given that up. We have turned over a new leaf. Now we want outer events to, by their "holiness," shine *purity* on our ego, to prove just how righteous and spiritual we are, how not-guilty we are.

The above two impulses are often at war with each other. The first may look upon the second as sanctimonious and unnecessarily sacrificing, which then looks back and sees the first as indulgent and "worldly." Yet both of them share perhaps the deepest and most insidious distortion of guidance. They both see guidance as being *primarily about form*. They both believe that the main role of the Holy Spirit is to tell us what to do, what to say, what house to buy, what job to take, etc. If, under this belief, we then make guidance the center of our spiritual path—as I think

14

some students do—then our path is nothing but a learning in how to deal with outer forms. It is not an exercise in awakening to God.

The Holy Spirit was sent to us with a higher mission than making sure our electric bill gets paid. His goal is to awaken us from the dream of a separate self surrounded by a world of form. Yet because we believe in electricity and electric bills, He makes a concession to that. He is willing to work within our belief, even though He knows that those things are just dream images. So He does work with the forms of our lives, but with one crucial stipulation: He works with them as *dream symbols.* Knowing they are just dream images, He knows that what is important is not the image itself, but what it symbolizes; not the form, but the meaning that we associate with it in our minds. For remember, His role is to heal our thinking. As a result, He is only interested in outer forms insofar as they affect the healing of our thinking. There are four points that I have found helpful in clarifying this basic idea:

1. In any situation, we must first seek to heal our minds, and only then seek for guidance on what to do.

This is one of the most difficult things to really practice about guidance. For the last thing most of us want to do is really change our minds. It is so much easier to skip over addressing our mental kinks and move on to fixing the problem "out there." Often I will find myself wondering what to do, while I am basically ignoring the knot of fear or resentment lying in my stomach. At that point my real job is to consciously stop and turn my attention away from what to do, for addressing and healing this knot is far more important than any set of outer conditions. This point is underscored powerfully in a message that Helen Schucman received which was not included in the Course:

You cannot ask, "What shall I say to him?" and hear God's answer. Rather ask instead, "Help me to see this brother through the eyes of truth and not of judgment," and the help of God and all His angels will respond.

(Absence from Felicity, Kenneth Wapnick, p. 396)

Besides the basic point that salvation is mind change, not physical change, there are two very concrete reasons to address first the healing of the mind. One is that behavior is really just a thought-reinforcer. No matter what behavior we perform, the effect which that behavior has on us will not be due to the form of the behavior itself. It will be solely a result of the *meaning* we see in that behavior, the purpose we invest in it. The behavior, being a reinforcer, will simply serve to strengthen whatever thought it was meant to express. So, if poisonous thinking is lurking in my mind, no matter what I do, my behavior will simply serve to express that poison and thereby increase the toxin count in my mind.

The other reason for addressing mind healing first is that you will probably only get the guidance you seek once you heal your mind. That knot of fear or resentment that I was talking about is lying in the channel through which the Holy Spirit speaks to you. It muffles His Voice. Even while you are asking Him, "What should I do?" that knot is saying to Him, "Get outta here. I want it my way!" Conversely, the appropriate behavior, being an expression of healed thinking, is part of that thinking. It naturally goes along with it. So once you heal your thinking, the way to express that new thinking will often occur to you quite easily. For just as water will naturally find a channel to flow through, so love, once present, will find the way it wants to flow out of you.

2. The most important guidance to receive is on how to look at a situation.

We know, at least intellectually, that we should look upon every situation with the eyes of forgiveness and love. So why do we need the Holy Spirit to tell us how to look at a situation? Because it is often not enough to know that we should be loving. We need a specific way of looking at it that will unlock the love in us. In your own path, and if you have ever helped someone with their path, you most likely have found that it is simply not good enough to say, "Just forgive." Instead, you must find the particular perspective that, like a key, perfectly fits the lock in your mind and thus can open it. Maybe it's, "You resent her because you see your mother in her," or, "You were depending on her because you don't acknowledge the light in you," or, "The gift she was sent to bring you is so much more important than her ego." This kind of guidance is far more valuable than telling you what to do behaviorally. And, conversely, guidance on what you should do will often obviously imply the right way of looking at the situation. It is a form that suggests or implies healed content. Either way, the important thing is that we get our minds, not our bodies, in the right place.

3. What matters is not the right behavior, but the right-mindedness behind it.

This goes along with the above. Yet it deserves separate mention, for it is particularly important and especially difficult, at least in my experience. From my point of view, this is a basic cornerstone of what you could call the "Course lifestyle." What it really means is that we should act out of love for others, rather than out of a concern for the right forms. In other words, the content of love is more important than any form. The dreamer is more important than the dream.

This message has been one that the small community I am part of has been given repeatedly. As I mentioned, Sandy, one of our members, possesses what we have grown to consider a very helpful channel to the Holy Spirit. As we have turned to this source for help with our community issues, we have repeatedly been surprised with the message that it is not the form that matters, but only the love. The number of times we have had to be told this is almost embarrassing. We asked how long should our meetings be and were told, "Be not bound to time as a measure of success, but rather to the quality of your togetherness." One of our members gave all his money to a man who claimed that he and his family were destitute and living off of "ketchup soup." We asked if the man was for real or not and were told that that was "irrelevant." The important thing was not "the circumstances of the situation," but that our friend "extended love in the best way he knew how."

We have constantly gotten into arguments over decisions. At one point we were told, "Let go of an idea if it stands between you and your brother." But we did not listen. We argued about what God's will is and then asked for confirmation on our decision. We were told, "If something is pulling you apart, force not that thing. My will is for you to love each other...." We argued about what to do with a large sum of money we were given and then asked for confirmation of that decision. We were told, "Has your process been a loving one?...If the process is pure, the outcome will work itself out. Look not to the end result to determine 'success' or 'failure.' Your minds must be trained away from this, and must dwell in the love that you have for one another." We even argued about guidelines for when to turn to this source of guidance, and then turned to it for confirmation of the guidelines we devised. This was our answer:

> You need be more concerned with the way you treat each other than with specific rules or guidelines. The guidelines are set up to help you receive guidance, which will tell you to

love each other. Do not violate this guideline, the only lasting and important one.

As you can see, we have been a little slow on the uptake about this. In the face of "real" issues and decisions this idea can seem irrelevant and even infuriating. From this experience I have learned just how stubbornly resistant to love we humans are, and how fiercely attached to forms. After many years my friends and I are still struggling to accept the priority of love over forms. And I have learned that attachment to the "right" forms is not only not love, it is the enemy of love. For in the end you care more about the forms than the people, and you end up attacking the people to preserve the forms.

4. The Holy Spirit's guidance and supply do not really complete us. They are just dream symbols of God's changeless Love and of our pre-existing completeness in Heaven.

It is so easy to fall into thinking that when we get answers or physical supply from the Holy Spirit that those things actually fill a real lack in us. Yet that is the ego's way of thinking, that we are actually little empty beings who can be completed by accumulating physical and mental forms from outside of us.

Instead, we need to mentally de-emphasize the form of the answer or bit of supply we receive. We need to realize that of itself it is really nothing. This is stated very clearly at one point in the Course, where we are told that the Holy Spirit "will supply [our needs] with no emphasis at all upon them" (Text, p. 239; T-13.VII.13:2). Now, my first tendency when I get supplied is to dance around the house—not exactly the "of course" attitude being described here. Then, in *The Song of Prayer*, the point is made more fully:

> The form of the answer, if given by God, will suit your need as you see it. This is merely an echo of the reply of His Voice.

The real sound is always a song of thanksgiving and of love....In true prayer you hear only the song. All the rest is merely added. You have sought first the Kingdom of Heaven, and all else has indeed been given you. (Song of Prayer, p. 2)

In other words, when we receive some mental or physical form from the Holy Spirit, its real significance lies in its being a dream symbol of the infinite fullness we already possess in Heaven, a visible symbol of the formless Love that pours unceasingly from God to us. Of itself it is nothing, but as a symbol it is wonderful. It is like we are children coming to our Mommy with an imaginary hurt, asking her to kiss the hurt. Being a loving Mommy, she kisses it. She knows full well she is filling a "need" we just made up, yet she wants to communicate love to us in a form we can understand.

The real benefits of being guided

Guidance, then, is real, but it needs to be reframed. We need to see it not as the Holy Spirit's taking care of our outer affairs, but as a vital aspect of spiritual awakening. The following are some of the benefits of living a guided life.

1. Ego relinquishment.

One of the ego's main stomping grounds is its act of running our lives. On the surface, we want to run our own lives because we think we can do it better than anyone else. Yet, on a more basic level, we simply want the *feeling* of being in control. It is not just the results of our control that we want, it is the control itself. It is its own end. It is pure, undiluted ego elixir.

The idea that we are in charge of our existence is an offspring of the idea that we are in charge of our being, that we created ourselves. It is a reflection of the original attempt to usurp God's function as Creator. At the core of the ego is the idea of self-sufficiency, that this "tiny self of one alone against the universe" (Psychotherapy, p. 15) is completely independent, sufficient unto itself; that parts of reality can be "wrested from the whole and seen as separate and wholes within themselves" (Workbook, p. 251; W-pI.136.6:3).

By trying to guide and supply ourselves, we are reflecting this basic thought of self-sufficiency. Very simply, we are trying to usurp God's function as our Source. We are attempting to be our own source. And so, by letting the Holy Spirit run the show, by returning the function of guidance and supply to Whom it really belongs, we are knocking out a basic pillar of our egos.

2. The cleansing of guilt.

This point is an extension of the point above. Something inside of us knows very well that it is our Source Who is supposed to direct us and supply us with all we need. And so when we take the function of guidance and supply to ourselves, we feel guilty, as if we have stolen fire from Heaven. *The Psychotherapy* pamphlet points out that when we feel we are in charge, we are regarding ourselves as "self-created rather than God-created" (Psychotherapy, p. 14). Thus, it says, "Guilt is inevitable in those who use their judgment in making their decisions" (Psychotherapy, p. 14). The Manual puts it very clearly:

> To follow the Holy Spirit's guidance is to let yourself be absolved of guilt. It is the essence of the Atonement. It is the core of the curriculum. The imagined usurping of functions not your own is the basis of fear. The whole world you see reflects the illusion that you have done so, making fear inevitable. To return the function to the One to Whom it belongs is thus the escape from fear. And it is this that lets the memory of love return to you. Do not, then, think that following the Holy Spirit's guidance is necessary merely because of your own inadequacies. It is the way out of hell for you.
>
> (Manual, p. 67; M-29.3:3-11)

To put this more simply, there is an incredible release that comes from feeling like you are not responsible. Of course you are responsible, but the best way to use your responsibility is to turn it over to the Holy Spirit. At that point, whatever happens is on His head, so to speak, not yours. What a relief! This truth can be misused, of course. But the fact that it can be misused does not take away from the fact that it is a genuine and transformative fact of life.

3. Things work better.

In my experience, once you have really turned things over and are in tune with the Holy Spirit, things just go better, and without your having to work as hard. The fact is, the Holy Spirit is simply a lot better at arranging things than you are. And He will actually arrange things for you, taking care of affairs that you would have had to accomplish by your own sweat before.

This is a point I can really appreciate, leaning, as I have since birth, toward the lethargic side. I personally know of no better labor-saving device than simply staying in tune and letting the river do the work. Your only alternative is to do the work yourself *while* you are paddling against the flow of the river. And, of course, this is how most of us go through life, trying to constantly pressure things into fitting our expectations, as well as anticipate what is around the bend, while all the while disregarding the way things want to flow. Not only does this take more effort and produce more stress, it just does not get the results. True, a few people seem really good at getting their way, but even those few do so at the cost of their peace of mind.

In contrast, the Holy Spirit will literally carry you along, if you let Him. The following well-known passage beautifully captures this sense of being carried along:

Once you accept His plan as the one function that you would fulfill, there will be nothing else the Holy Spirit will not arrange for you without your effort. He will go before you making straight your path, and leaving in your way no stones to trip on, and no obstacles to bar your way. Nothing you need will be denied you. Not one seeming difficulty but will melt away before you reach it. You need take thought for nothing, careless of everything except the only purpose that you would fulfill. (Text, p. 404; T-20.IV.8:4-8)

Of course, it is important to see this in the right framework, as discussed in point #4 of the previous section. We must see it not as the Holy Spirit shoring up our greedy (and lazy) egos, but as the Holy Spirit providing us with lots of dream symbols of the pre-existing fullness and ease of our reality in Heaven.

4. Frees up time, energy and belief for higher pursuits.

This is clearly an extension of the above point. It is one that I personally would not have thought of, yet it comes through very clearly in the private guidance which Helen Schucman received:

The reason I direct everything that is unimportant is because it is no way to waste your free will. If you insist on doing the trivial your way, you waste too much time and will on it. Will cannot be free if it is tied up in trivia. It never gets out.

I will tell you exactly what to do in connection with everything that does not matter. That is not an area where choice should be invested. There is better use of time.

You have to remember to ask Me to take charge of all minutiae, and they will be taken care of so well and so quickly that you cannot bog down in it.

The only remaining problem is that you will be unwilling to ask because you are afraid *not* to be bogged down. Do not let this hold us back. If you will ask, I can arrange these things even if you are not too enthusiastic.

(Absence from Felicity, Kenneth Wapnick, p. 235)

This guidance is clear in saying that Jesus will, by taking care of physical things for us, free up time and energy that we can then use for God. But one also gets the impression that this will also free our minds from being so entrenched in the reality of form. This makes a great deal of sense to me. The more that we have to use our time and energy to muck around with "trivia" and "minutiae," the more we will come to believe in the reality of such things, and, by extension, the reality of this whole trivial, minute realm.

5. His choice of forms symbolizes His way of thinking.

This point has been alluded to already—that the Holy Spirit's answers tend to clearly imply His way of looking at things and therefore put us in touch with His Mind. It is true that form is not content, but it is also true that you can get to know fairly reliably what someone is thinking by what behaviors he chooses. This is true for humans as well as for the Holy Spirit. Through being exposed over and over to His behavioral answers, you end up getting a good feel for how He thinks about things, how His Mind works.

I find, for instance, that the Holy Spirit's answers in form generally communicate a profound reliance on the unseen, on the unseen power of the Spirit, and on the unseen light within other people. Following such guidance either transforms your thinking, or it creates a lot of stress and anxiety inside. In other words, if you are repeatedly led to do things in the world that only make sense if you are trusting in some force of purity and goodness in other people and in some Higher Power to hold you up, then that has an effect on you. It puts you in touch very concretely with the Holy Spirit's way of thinking; it puts a certain internal pressure on you to adopt that thinking yourself, since you are committing your actions to it; and it gives you an opportunity to see whether or not that thinking bears real fruit.

The place of guidance on the path

We are now, I hope, in a position to see what place guidance actually has on the spiritual path. There are two common positions that I believe are incorrect and serve, by contrast, to highlight the position I am trying to describe:

The Holy Spirit simply guides you into the proper forms. This, of course, is the conventional image of guidance. Yet, who cares about just parroting the right forms? What point is there unless it wakes you up?

Guidance is not very relevant to the spiritual life. This is an extreme position, but it captures a sentiment that I hear fairly often. The idea is that since it is the content of our thinking that matters, not the forms we engage in, being guided in our outer lives is not all that relevant to mind change. Hence, when it comes to those forms, we should just use our own common sense.

However, common sense is generally ego-sense. If I am playing the manager of my life, then I am expressing ego. And what I express I reinforce.

What I believe the correct position to be incorporates the truth within each one of the above. That position is that guidance is not the center of the spiritual path; it is not the primary engine of awakening. Yet, it is an authentic part of real spiritual awakening, because it is not primarily about outer direction, but about inner transformation. It is its own form of yoga. Through being guided, I relinquish the control that I have given my ego and transfer power and authority to a higher Presence within me. I learn how that Presence sees things and I learn that It is trustable and that It loves me. And I allow It to fill my journey through time and space with dream symbols of the grace, effortlessness and fullness in which my Self abides in Heaven.

CHAPTER 3

The Proper Mental Set

Perhaps the most important thing we can do toward the reception of clear, reliable, consistent guidance is to cultivate the proper mental set. This is a kind of overall attitude toward the Holy Spirit, ourselves and our lives. This cultivation is really like building a healthy soil in the garden. The more rich and healthy this soil becomes, the more naturally and effortlessly will the plant of genuine guidance emerge from it.

Proper attitude toward ourselves

First, we will discuss the proper attitude toward ourselves, an attitude which begins with a profound humility when it comes to our own powers.

In my experience, extreme open-mindedness is almost the key attitude in the whole enterprise of receiving guidance. In fact, the Course calls open-mindedness, or the giving up of judgment, "the obvious prerequisite for hearing God's Voice" (Manual, p. 25; M-9.2:4). Fixed ideas about what things are, what should happen, how things should go, are the enemies of guidance. Over and over again I have seen real guidance knock up against the fixed ideas in my mind or in someone else's mind, resulting in pain as it feels almost like an animal is clawing at our bodies. If our ideas cause such turbulence when guidance is present, imagine how much guidance they block from ever making it to awareness.

It is an absolute key in receiving guidance to cultivate over time an habitual humility about our own mental powers. It must become second nature to us that we just do not know. Not only do we not know what reality is, who we are or who anyone else is, we don't even know the relevant information for making the decision that lies in front of us. We don't have enough intelligence to use that information, even if we had it. We don't know the relevant alternatives that are facing us, nor the outcomes of each alternative that we do know, nor the overall future that awaits us. And even if we did know all these things, we don't have the proper priorities—the absolute love toward ourselves and toward everyone else involved—that would make our judgment wise, healthy and fair. Therefore, in and of ourselves, *we just do not know what to do.*

Intimately associated with this open-mindedness is detachment from outcomes, an absence of self-made agendas. By this I mean an inner willingness to go with any alternative that may prove guided. Normally, there are certain things which from our point of view just *have* to happen. It is as if we are trees that send mental roots into certain outcomes, certain conditions, rooting ourselves into those outcomes. Yet, if we plant ourselves in this field, and the Holy Spirit wants us over the hill from here, we are in trouble. Not only will we resist His guidance, we probably will not even allow it into awareness. We need to systematically pull our roots out of the little plot in which we have planted ourselves. We must mentally uproot ourselves so that we float free, suspended in the air, and thus can easily glide wherever the Holy Spirit would have us go. To be poised for guidance we must be flexible, fluid, ready to change course on a dime. Attachment to outcomes is mental baggage—the more we have, the harder it is to travel.

Obviously, one does not become open-minded and detached from outcomes overnight. It is part of the whole spiritual process of undoing the ego, for the ego is made of "certainties" and agendas, things that have to be true and things that have to happen. Attaining true humility is a result of day-in and day-out ego-emptying. It comes out of the constant practice of "I don't know": I don't know what's true and I don't know what's best for me.

So we must cultivate a deep realization of our inability to guide ourselves, a profound emptiness when it comes to our ability to lead. Yet we must develop an equally deep and implicit trust in our ability to follow. We must learn to trust our ability to let guidance through, our sensitivity to recognize it when it comes and our willingness to move with it, to follow it. At one point, the Course tells us,

> Trust not your good intentions. They are not enough. But trust implicitly your willingness, whatever else may enter. Concentrate only on this, and be not disturbed that shadows ["bad" intentions] surround it. (Text, p. 355; T-18.IV.2:1-4)

What this is saying, I believe, is that your thinking is not yet pure enough to be the guiding force behind the process. Yet, even though you cannot lead, there is something in you pure enough to enable you to *follow:* to allow the light through, to recognize the light when it shines on you and to walk in its direction. Whether you choose to do this or not, that is another matter. The fact is, though, that you are fully able to. There is a spark in you that will yield to the greater light. Trust this spark in you. Count on it. Rely on it. Know that it will be there like you know the sun will rise tomorrow.

Within this overall attitude toward ourselves as the bungling leader but gifted follower, we need to add at least one more component. We must believe that we deserve the Holy Spirit's guidance, that we deserve, in fact, everything that He has to give. Approaching Him as if He is unwilling to give to us is not only a belittling of ourselves, it is an accusation that He does not love us. And both of these things block our ability to receive from Him. I will return to this theme in the next chapter.

Proper attitude toward the Holy Spirit

If we were to carry only the above attitude toward ourselves, life would get pretty depressing. For the above is essentially a child-like attitude. And a child left without a parent, abandoned and alone, is lost. The Holy Spirit, then, is the other half of the equation. Where we are inadequate, He is perfectly capable. Where we are suited to follow, He is suited to lead. As we discussed in chapter 1, He is the perfect inner Parent.

Our attitude, then, needs to reflect all that was said about Him in chapter 1. We need to have the awareness that He does have all the relevant information, that He does have the intelligence to put it together, that He does see all the alternatives and know the outcome of each one, that He does have absolute love toward us and toward everyone involved, and that He does not withhold His gifts, since His only desire is to give to us. We need to look to Him with the same unquestioned trust with which a healthy three year-old would look to the most loving parent imaginable.

An important part of this is desire for the Holy Spirit's guidance. We must really want it, more than we want our own ideas, plans and fantasies of what our life should be. I have become convinced that, in the end, the sheer desire for guidance does more good than specific abilities, like hearing an inner voice. The person that really wants guidance will be the person that gets it and benefits from it.

Another part of this, of course, is faith and trust in the Holy Spirit. And this, for most of us, is a very tall order. In my experience, this kind of faith and trust simply cannot be manufactured, not if it is going to be truly realistic and mature. And, luckily, it is okay if we do not really trust the Holy Spirit right now. Such trust is something that generally develops over time. I am sure it can be born full-blown from within in an instant. But in my experience it has to develop over many years from countless life experiences, from repeatedly taking the "risk" and turning over to Him ever-new things and seeing what happens. Only by watching the Holy Spirit care for us over and over will we really be convinced deep down that He can be trusted with our lives, our hearts and our souls.

In the meantime, I personally feel that an experimental attitude is the most honest and healthy posture that we can take. This attitude says, "I don't really know if I can trust the Holy Spirit. But I also don't know that I cannot. It may in fact be true that He gives only good and that all my pain has come from me. Therefore, I am open and willing to learn. I'll give it a genuine try and see what happens." I really think this honest attitude is preferable to both close-minded skepticism and to whipped up, artificial "faith."

In the end, though, our trust in the Holy Spirit must become an habitual part of our mental framework, in the same way that a child's whole mind is soaked through with reliance on its parents. We must walk around not even having to think about the fact that for every situation the Holy Spirit has the most brilliant and wonderful plan just waiting—like water pooled on the top of a tent—to come splashing down on us. Just as we can sense the ceiling above us without having to look up at it, so we must sense His plan poised above us, without having to consciously think about it. And just as we generally carry a non-specific anxiety born of our anticipation of future threat, so we must instead carry a non-specific thrill, born of our anticipation of the Holy Spirit's gifts. We must go through our day feeling our whole being resting in His hands, feeling ourselves leaning back on Him in total relaxation and security, knowing that He has taken care of everything. And out of all of this must come a deep-running gratitude, a sacred sense that we could never repay Him for the gifts He has given; a sense that sometimes overflows into conscious emotion, but most of the time abides as a general mental buoyancy, an overall sustaining force.

Both inside and outside

The above distinction between child and Parent, which seems so neat and tidy, does get a little blurry when you consider the fact that He is an *inner* Parent. This complicates things quite a bit, and not just theoretically. How we conceive of the Holy Spirit's within-ness vs. without-ness has heavy practical consequences. I do not pretend to fully understand this issue, but the following is what I think I understand at the present time.

He is outside our personal mental machinery.

I think it is essential to have a very healthy respect for the enormous difference between the Holy Spirit and your personal mental machinery, your conscious will, intelligence and feeling. Your current powers of reasoning are what the ego has left you after shutting out the vast majority of your reason. And even this tiny remnant is almost totally dominated by the ego. Thus, your own self-generated ideas and feelings are not the Holy Spirit;

they are the very thing that He is the correction for.

And this does not just mean your conscious mind. Level after level of your mind, extending into vast unconscious regions, are choked with the ego's garbage. Since guidance has to wade through all that stuff to get to you, it generally comes infrequently and is usually limited and distorted. God always gives, but we are often blocked to receiving.

Thus, guidance is not whatever feeling or whim happens to be crossing your mind at the moment. It may not even be your best intuitions. I recall many examples of guidance directly overturning seemingly clear intuitions. In one case, my household was about to move out to Sedona and we all sat down and tuned into our feelings of what living situation we should be moving into. The four of us were unanimous in deciding that we needed separate dwellings that were still in close proximity. Yet when we got out here we happened into a living situation so serendipitously that it was clearly exactly what the Holy Spirit intended. Yet, sure enough, it put us all in the same house again, and even added on a fifth person. So much for our intuitions!

He is inside our minds.

The other side of the above, however, is the fact that the Holy Spirit is definitely inside our minds. This means that many of our conscious thoughts and feelings are not self-generated. They may seem to be cranked out by our own conscious machinery, but they are actually little rays of the Holy Spirit's light shining through the spaces between the gears. In fact, because the Holy Spirit is in our minds, we always already know His answer—if we are willing to admit it to ourselves. Sometimes this answer is so buried that, realistically, we will not be able to uncover it right now. Yet quite often it is right there in the back of our minds, yet we turn our eyes away from it.

I have talked to people facing decisions many times when it

was clear that they knew full well what the answer was, and that their talking it out with me was both an expression of their desire to find the answer and an expression of their denial and avoidance of what they already knew. I remember one experience I had in which I really wanted to use some unexpected money for something altruistic, but also wondered if perhaps I should not use it to take a trip and see a sort of earthly "elder brother" of mine. I sat down and talked it out with a friend, trying to spill my mind and search my feelings. And the more I talked about it, the more the "altruistic" use of the money felt totally forced and dead, and the more the trip idea felt glowing with aliveness. The answer was already in my mind, just needing to be uncovered.

Thus, the Holy Spirit's guidance is both the bolts of lightning that come out of the blue and take us by complete surprise and the inner knowings that have been rolling around in our minds for years. Similarly, we must have the humility to realize that our every whim is not straight from the throne of God, while at the same time having the sense of worth and dignity to accept the fact that Holiness is woven like a golden thread throughout our very own thoughts and feelings.

CHAPTER 4

Receiving the Guidance

Now that we have erected a certain context for the receiving of guidance, let us turn our attention to the actual process and experience of seeking and receiving it.

Forms of guidance

I think most all of us know that there are many forms of guidance. The most common conventional image is that of hearing an inner voice. Yet hearing a voice is just one form of guidance, with some unique advantages as well as some disadvantages. In my own mind I have classified forms of guidance into two categories: inner and outer.

Inner guidance includes intuitions, impressions, hunches, inner voices, internal imagery, dreams, etc.—all those ways in which something shows up in our minds that we conclude in some way came from His Mind. Within this overall category, though, I think there are two sub-categories: direct and indirect. *Direct* includes intuitions, impressions, feelings—instances in which our minds directly and somewhat formlessly feel the meaning conveyed. *Indirect* includes words, images and dreams—instances in which the meaning may be felt somewhat directly, but is also conveyed by some form or symbol which must be interpreted and which seems to have come from outside our conscious minds.

My belief is that what I am calling intuitions, impressions and feelings—all of which I personally refer to as intuition—are the most important form of guidance. For if we are directly feeling an idea from the Holy Spirit, then we are sharing a thought with Him. In other words, a union has occurred between our minds and the Holy Spirit's. And this is really the goal of guidance: to unite our minds with the Holy Spirit's so that there is no longer any difference between our thoughts and His thoughts, our feelings and His feelings.

This explains a phenomenon that initially puzzled me. When my friend, Sandy, began receiving inner guidance, she would repeatedly ask it a question, only to be told to "look within." At this point, one's natural temptation would be to reply, "I *am* looking within. Why do you think I was asking You?" After a time, though, it became clear that there was wisdom behind the reply she received. Rather than passing on words to a passive recipient, this inner Voice wanted that recipient to unite with It on a feeling level. This is why It urged her to find guidance in the form of her intuition.

Yet because we are not always willing or ready to unite with the Holy Spirit, intuition is often the most personally-colored form of guidance. So, for instance, if some idea is totally outside our conscious framework, it may have to find its way to us through another form of guidance. At one point in the Course, Jesus says, "No one can see through a wall, but I can step around it" (Text, p. 56; T-4.III.7:4). I see inspired intuition as a case where we have decided to take the wall down and join with what is on the other side. But where the wall remains up, I think that guidance has to step around it and come to us in other forms; for instance, in the forms of inner voices and images.

These other forms can be a great blessing, though. Although I think that someday they will pass away in favor of a total union of our minds and the Holy Spirit's Mind, for now they are wonderful because they can bring to us truths that are very alien to our whole conscious mental framework—something that intuition will not do as often (unless you are one of the few that possess a powerful intuition that can reach far beyond your own conscious mind).

This brings us to outer forms of guidance. If the Spirit cannot tell us all that He has to say through inner voices and images, He turns to our "outer" lives. We all have experienced ways in which an outer event will seem to be a form of guidance. We open a book to the perfect place at the right moment; someone speaks just the right words to us; a song comes on the radio; a striking coincidence occurs. These outer events are in principle the same as inner voices or dreams, although, I believe, they are more indirect. Since the outer world is not really outer, but is just a dream, such signs, omens and synchronicities are really just dream symbols. They are like inspired dreams at night in which the Spirit seems to have shaped the images in our minds into messengers of His guidance.

Here again I think there are two sub-categories: spontaneous and divination. Divination includes Tarot, I Ching, tea leaves, casting lots, etc. In divination you set up a situation, a framework, inside of which you then set in motion some action. The results of the action, however, will not be under your conscious control. They will be "random," leaving room for a meaning beyond your conscious mind to come in and shape the results. You then interpret these results in order to find your answer. This is perhaps the most time-honored means of seeking guidance.

Under the spontaneous category are all those events that seem, as in divination, to have a meaningful pattern not placed there by human hands. Yet the difference in this case is that these patterns occur "naturally," spontaneously, unexpectedly; in the normal course of daily life, rather than in the midst of a situation that has been intentionally set up for the receiving of guidance. In this category are what has come to be called *synchronicities*, or coincidences, in which events with related meanings occur spontaneously together in time. Also in this category is what I like to call *parallels*, in which situations or personalities that may be separated in time and space inexplicably display striking parallels.

Overall, I think that the Spirit would like to reach us through intuition, through the union of our minds and His. However, if there are things we are unable to receive in that way, He turns to inner words and images. Or He dreams His answers into our "outer" dream. All methods need to be valued, however. Until we fully awaken the indirect methods will remain valuable, for through them the Holy Spirit can communicate things that are more alien to our current mental framework.

Normal operating procedure

Guidance, I believe, needs to be more than an occasional seeking of answers. It needs to be a moment-by-moment act of staying in the flow. While travelling at sea, you do not let the ship go wherever it wants to and then every few days try to ascertain the direction in which you should be heading. So, by "normal operating procedure" I mean, "How do we go through each day and each hour in such a way that keeps us in the flow?"

The bottom line, I believe, is, we practice our spiritual path.

We put in the time, day-in and day-out, to give our egos over to the Holy Spirit. On a level more specifically relevant to guidance, we cultivate the mental set discussed in chapter 3; that of being a child who is unsuited to lead but who is a great follower, and who is overshadowed by a Parent Who is the perfect, loving Leader.

Our spiritual practice is, I believe, the most important thing we can do in order to elicit guidance. For most guidance is an automatic response to thinking in line with the Holy Spirit. In fact, I think that most guidance is simply unconscious. It is neither consciously sought nor consciously received. Turning our thinking over to the Holy Spirit has allowed Him to, in some sense, just take over. Look at the following passage from the Text:

> My control can take over everything that does not matter, while my guidance can direct everything that does, if you so choose....behavior...is controlled by me automatically as soon as you place what you think under my guidance.
>
> (Text, p. 25; T-2.VI.1:3, 2:8-9)

What Jesus is saying here is that he will guide what does matter, which is our *thinking*, while he will *control* what does not matter, which is our *behavior*. And that giving him permission to guide simultaneously gives permission to control. In other words, if you allow him to guide your thinking, he will just come in and take over your behavior! This is strongly stated, but I think this is the way it actually happens. So often we find ourselves in the perfect place at the perfect time. How did we get there? We were not aware of making choices for the sake of arriving at this destination. Someone must have been pulling the strings in us without our knowing it.

Yet normal operating procedure, I believe, also means the conscious seeking of guidance. I see this seeking as two-fold: *constantly asking and constantly consulting our intuition*. In terms of asking, let us look at what I think is the most practical thing the Course has to say about guidance:

> Does this mean that you cannot say anything without consulting Him? No, indeed! That would hardly be practical, and it is the practical with which this course is most concerned. If you have made it a habit to ask for help when and where you can, you can be confident that wisdom will be given you when you need it. Prepare for this each morning, remember God when you can throughout the day, ask the Holy Spirit's help when it is feasible to do so, and thank Him for His guidance at night. And your confidence will be well founded indeed.
>
> (Manual, p. 68; M-29.5:5-10)

This passage says a world. First it says that you need not ask for nor be conscious of receiving specific guidance on every little thing, for that would be impractical. What you should do is:

1. Ask for help whenever you can.

Asking for help is mentioned twice and each time is qualified: "when and where you can," "when it is feasible...."

2. Do your spiritual practice.

The lines about preparing each morning, remembering God throughout the day and thanking Him at night are really a reference to the Course's formula for practice as outlined in the Workbook.

If you do this, then, "wisdom will be given you when you need it." This is an important line. Rather than specific words, you will receive "wisdom"—suggesting perhaps more of a formless, inner knowing. And rather than the guidance coming immediately, it will come "when you need it." Thus, the overall impression given is that we should just do our practice and frequently ask for help, and somehow, at some time, our thoughts and actions will be informed by a higher Wisdom.

This is not the only place in the Course where the habit of

frequent asking is urged. In another place you are urged to, at the beginning of each hour,

> ...quietly sit by and wait on Him and listen to His Voice, and learn what He would have us do the hour that is yet to come; while thanking Him for all the gifts He gave us in the one gone by. (Workbook, p. 279; W-pI.153.17:2)

The point is to just keep asking. Whenever you are faced with uncertainty or perplexity, just say, "Holy Spirit help me with this." And as much as possible do not exclude any area of your life from this asking. Each time you invite the Holy Spirit in it is a statement that you want Him in all areas. Each time you exclude Him it is a statement that you want Him out completely. For this reason, we are urged repeatedly in the Workbook to exclude nothing from our practice, just as in the private guidance that Helen Schucman received (as recorded in *Absence from Felicity*), she and Bill Thetford were urged repeatedly to ask Jesus about *everything*.

Whereas by "constantly asking," I mean handing up requests for help to the Holy Spirit without expecting any particular immediate results, by "constantly consulting our intuition," I mean something slightly different. There, we tune into the highest, truest sense within us of what we should do and how we should view things. There we are looking for immediate results.

I personally think that this process of staying in touch with our intuition is an extremely important one. Several years ago, in order to make consulting my intuitions a habit, I spent a year training myself. I recorded each day how many times I asked my intuition and how many times I followed what I got. And then I charted it all on a graph over the months. It was a pretty cumbersome discipline, but it made staying in touch with my intuition a permanent habit. For me, spending less than a minute feeling for my highest inner sense of things can give me an entirely new outlook on something. I still do it several times a day, when I reach points at which I am uncertain or at which I suspect that my intuition would differ with my conscious tendencies. It has proved to be an invaluable practice.

However, I personally do not trust my intuitions very far, as I do not feel extremely developed in my union with the Holy Spirit. I have found my intuitions to be very colored by my own way of thinking and limited by the range of my information. So I use intuition to guide me in little matters, or when it seems pretty clear what to do. But in larger matters, especially when I sense that things could go one of many ways, I often wait for or rely on an instance in which I can be relatively sure that the Spirit has spoken.

When the Spirit speaks

Whereas we can always ask for help and intuition can be consulted at any time, the appearance of genuine, reliable, incontrovertible guidance is more rare. It is as if there hasn't been a cloud in the sky for weeks, or months, or even years; the plants are dry and the ground is hard. Then suddenly, without warning, thunderclouds form overhead and rain comes pouring down amid a fireworks show of lightning.

This is how I, and I think many people, experience guidance. I have been plodding along on my intuition and some minor signs and then suddenly, out of the clear blue sky, I get hit by a shower of guidance, inner and outer, all of it with a unity of underlying themes and a network of revealing interconnections. For a day or so it just keeps coming. I find those times very exciting. I feel like a farmer must feel when the drought is punctuated by a storm—like walking out in the rain and just feeling it splash on my upturned face.

This may not be exactly the way guidance turns up in your

life, but I think most people who have consciously experienced guidance have particular forms that have shown themselves to be genuine and reliable over time. For me, it is primarily outer signs. For someone else it may be an inner voice. For someone else it will be inspired dreams. For yet another person it will be a certain quality of inner knowing.

Each person has their own way, yet the fact remains that for all of us the times when the Spirit really speaks are beyond our control; they come unexpectedly. Like thunderstorms, they have a logic of their own that does not obey our rules. From our conscious perspective, they just seem to happen. In my experience, they happen at times that I am spiritually attuned and at times when my mind is in the gutter. It does not seem to matter. Even for people who hear an inner voice that they can turn on and off like a light switch, there will be special times when something truly marvelous and revelatory comes through. Even for people who receive help from their dreams every night, there will be the occasional "big dream."

When the Spirit speaks we need to pay special attention. These times are not normal operating procedure. And they should be given authority to illumine, reframe and even abrogate all that came through *during* normal operating procedure. For many people I am sure that it would not be helpful to get into analyzing these experiences. But if it does suit your temperament, I would suggest that you get everything that you can out of them. If and when it feels right, reflect on them, discuss them with friends, write about them, even draw them. I met an artist once who had a life-changing dream that he depicted in, I think, more than a dozen different paintings. For the fact is that there is *always* more meaning to be plumbed from these experiences. There is always so much more there than you first suspect.

By dwelling on and even "mining" these experiences, they

begin to shape and inform the guiding visions behind your life. They start providing the basis for how you think about your path, your lessons, your relationships and your purpose. And well they should. Nothing else should be given such authority to form the basis for your understanding of your current lifetime. If the guiding visions of your life grow mainly out of the soil of these special experiences, then they will be well founded indeed.

SEARCHING FOR AN ANSWER ON
A PARTICULAR TOPIC

In my experience, if you do all your homework—your spiritual practice, cultivation of the proper mind-set for receiving guidance, constant asking for help and constant consulting of intuition—guidance just comes when you need it. You do not often have to go through a lengthy process of seeking answers about a particular topic. Yet, I think that for most of us there will still be times in which such a process is very helpful, even necessary. So in the following pages I would like to outline a process of seeking for guidance. I intend to throw everything I can into this, which means that in actual practice you may only need to use a few of the things mentioned.

Finding the question

If you are going to go through a process like this, you may ask about whatever you like. For some it may be best to ask about something relatively minor, so that they can learn to work with guidance in an atmosphere in which the stakes are not too high. For others it may be best to ask about something fairly significant, something that affects much of their lives, like an important relationship, a job, a move, etc. Either way, it need not be something that requires a physical change; it may just need a change in perspective. Leave no area out of consideration. There may be some significant area that is dramatically affecting your whole state of mind, but which you would like to allow to run along as is. These are important things to confront. If you like, you may find it helpful to pick an area in your life right now and go through this process as you read.

Ask about the step in front of you.

This is important. A common mistake is to ask about some distant future that is more than one step in front of you. This means that you are not trusting the Holy Spirit to carry you all along the way and that you are trusting your own ability to fill in the gaps. So ask yourself, "Is this step facing me right now? Do I have to decide about it now?"

Identify the heart of your concern.

Go into your feelings of uncertainty and concern and try to clear away extraneous issues and questions that you have piled onto whatever is really concerning you. As much as possible, get down to the nub of it. I personally find that there is usually one thing that is on my mind.

Do not be overly specific.

This may sound like a contradiction of the above point, but it need not be. I think it is quite possible to ask the Holy Spirit's help on whatever you deem the heart of your concern to be, and at the same time realize that His answer may take all kinds of forms, even very unexpected ones, including seeing the heart of the matter differently and answering a question other than the one you posed. One of the most common experiences in receiving guidance is finding that you asked the wrong question, that your question was really an expression of the problem, rather than a pure motion toward the answer. This is explained very clearly in private guidance which Helen Schucman received:

Any specific question involves a large number of assumptions which inevitably limit the answer. A specific question is actually a decision about the kind of answer that is acceptable. The purpose of words is to limit, and by limiting, to make a vast area of experience more manageable. But that means more manageable by you.

(*Absence from Felicity*, Kenneth Wapnick, p. 466)

Use whatever words facilitate the right intent.

Remember, your words do not matter to the Holy Spirit, only "the prayer of the heart" (Manual, p. 51; M-21.1:4). Feel free to use any words, "or only one, or none at all" (Manual, p. 40; M-16.10:7). Use what works for you. If you feel like your words would make any self-respecting Catholic saint refuse to intercede for you, chances are you are using the ones that really suit you.

Mind healing and clearing before asking

Explore alternatives, gather relevant information.

I believe that guidance can cover for gaps in our awareness of the facts. And it very often identifies alternatives that we never suspected were possible. This is part of what guidance is all about. I recall that once my household asked which ingredients to add to complete a compost heap. Unbeknownst to the particular channel, we were given the exact ingredients that, according to the book, we were missing (so why didn't we look in the book?). One of the hallmarks of real guidance is that it fits with facts and anticipates events of which we are not aware.

Still, though, it can be helpful to learn all that you can. And it can be very helpful to brainstorm and generate a variety of alternatives. For guidance—even "outer" guidance—comes through our minds. If we see a limited range of alternatives, that is a block which it has to hurdle. Lacks in information represent gaps it has to jump. And so, maybe a little research is appropriate. Similarly, do some brainstorming. Be creative. Challenge and take down mental walls as to what is possible. Do it not as a way to figure out the decision, but as a way of clearing the mental channels in preparation for the Holy Spirit to come rushing through.

Let go of fears and agendas.

Our normal picture of any situation is built mostly out of fears and self-made agendas. In any decision we face, we generally have a list of conditions that our final choice must meet. For instance, if we are looking for a new job, we are probably carrying around a whole set of conditions for it to fulfill, including money, benefits, status, hours, field, location, etc. Whereas some of these may reflect the Holy Spirit's guidance, were we to receive it, we must be at least willing to question all of them. We must realize that this process of mentally building our future is, in essence, the very process we used to dissociate from God and build our own world. It is the ego in action.

The backside of all these goals and agendas are our fears. We have fears that our goals will not be fulfilled and fears that certain unthinkable things will happen. We are afraid of what will happen if we let the situation out of our control. Therefore, these fears are, at least in part, fears of turning control over to the Holy Spirit. They recoil from Him and shut Him out.

It is important, therefore, to be able to identify our agendas and our fears, even state them clearly in words, and then be willing to release them, or at least to honestly question them. There are many ways to identify these fears and agendas. We can ask ourselves, "What do I want to happen in this situation?" or "What am I afraid will happen if I let the Holy Spirit in?" Another method, which I have picked up from the Pathwork teachings (channeled through Eva Pierrakos), is to see if your question sinks into your mind and is accepted into your unconscious like a seed being planted in fertile soil, or if your question is rejected by something in your mind, almost like it is coughing up something that tastes bad. If you get that coughing up feeling, try to trace where it is coming from.

Undoing our fears and agendas is so central to receiving guidance, that at this point you may want to write them down. Write down all the things you think should happen and all the things you are afraid will happen, especially those things you fear may result from turning the whole situation over to the Holy Spirit. Then do your best to question the validity of these fears and agendas and let them go into the Holy Spirit's hands.

Detach from outer outcomes, value inner awakening and love for others.

Most of the time we place our main value on the outer form of a situation. This means that we are really placing value on how well that form can please our egos. Instead, we must value the inner side, which consists of our own growth and awakening, and that of everyone else involved. That is all that matters. See the situation as a classroom in which you learn your lesson by attaining a loving intent toward everyone else in the classroom. Shift your values, then, from looking for better forms, to looking for the experience of God, in whatever form that may come.

Open your mind.

Become child-like. Realize how little you know, how different the answer may be from what you think, how vast is the real constellation of factors involved. Remember that, in comparison to the Holy Spirit's Mind, your mind is about as big as an ant's.

Asking

Now that you have laid all this groundwork, you are ready to ask. It may be that by this time this step has become unnecessary.

Simply by searching your feelings and discarding your blocks and agendas you may have come upon a clear knowing of what to do. Yet, even if you feel you are clear, you may want to ask for confirmation.

Ask with faith and confidence.

This is absolutely crucial. Faith and confidence are learned and so cannot simply be whipped up. Yet, if they are not strong, at least (as we said in chapter 3) you can have an experimental attitude of honest openness to the possibility that they are fully warranted.

Faith and confidence are founded on two critical beliefs. First, you must believe that you really and truly deserve the Holy Spirit's gifts. You must know that you are fully worthy of everything He has to give. Second, you must also believe that the Holy Spirit really wants to give to you, that, in fact, He yearns for you to receive His love, that saving you is the only purpose He has.

This theme of asking with faith and confidence is described in different ways by the Course material. For one, it is very potently stated in *The Song of Prayer*.

> Prayer...is not merely a question or an entreaty. It cannot succeed until you realize that it asks for nothing....True prayer must avoid the pitfall of asking to entreat. Ask, rather to receive what is already given; to accept what is already there.
>
> (Song of Prayer, p. 1)

In other words, God has already given you everything, including, in the Holy Spirit, every answer you ever needed and will ever need until the end of time. Why, then, would you beg for guidance, or for anything from God?

If one looks at the prayers included in the Course (most of them are in part II of the Workbook), one can get a very good feel for the attitude in which we should approach prayer. There is not a shred of timidity in these prayers. Everything is stated with confidence and without hesitation. It is implicitly assumed that all of God's gifts are ours. Thus, although there are many "thank you's," there is not one "please."

One of the lines that has been helpful to me comes from Helen and Bill's private guidance. Jesus here is speaking about Bill's asking for guidance:

> He doesn't have much real confidence that I will get through. He never just claims his rights. He should begin with much more confidence. I'll keep my promises...
>
> (*Absence from Felicity*, Kenneth Wapnick, p. 197)

A friend of a friend once told me that she was very talented at manifesting things. What she said about how she does it really struck me. She said that she gets into a state of mind in which *asking and receiving are one and the same thing*, in which the asking *is* the receiving. She said that when she gets into that state, dramatic results often follow almost immediately.

So ask with this kind of attitude. Know that your worth and the Holy Spirit's love join together in making the answer completely yours. Know that it has already been yours since the dawn of time and simply awaits your acceptance.

Ask with desire.

Get in touch with your desire for the answer. Feel the beauty of being in contact with the Spirit of God and know that happiness is all that He gives. If, as you seek to contact your desire, you find your mind recoiling, identify the fear and seek to release it.

Ask with willingness.

Remember that the Holy Spirit knows far better than you how you can find your way to the other side of the jungle, where happiness awaits you. In this light, ask with the willingness to yield to His answer when it comes, to follow wherever He would lead, whether that means making mental changes or physical changes or both. Again, if you find your mind recoiling, find the cause and seek healing for it.

Let it go into His hands.

Your answer may have popped into your head as soon as you asked. But if not, do not hang onto the question anymore. Don't feel that giving the question to the Holy Spirit is like leaving your kids with a baby sitter you don't trust. If you hang onto the question then you do not think it has been left in reliable hands. Let it go, knowing that it is in the most capable hands possible.

Thank Him for the answer.

Whether you are aware of the answer or not, the fact is that the answer has been given. The check really is in the mail. So thank the Holy Spirit for what He has given. In so doing, you affirm that it already is yours.

Have a sense of anticipation.

Be confident that the answer will appear at the right time. Even have an excitement about the prospect of touching a Mind higher than yours, about seeing through the mire of your mental swamp to a bit of the real truth.

Awaiting the answer

Realize it may take time and may come in unexpected forms.

Sometimes answers will come after quite a while. I do not think the Holy Spirit actually waits; the delay comes from our own blocks. So the answer may take time. For this reason, if you asked about a decision facing you, try to hold off on deciding until the guidance comes. Also, it may come in forms that seem unrelated to the question. In fact, I once read that the answer to a prayer may initially come as a healing of what is blocking the actual thing that you asked for.

Do not assume that He has forgotten.

If your hope of getting an answer has lagged, do what you

can to rekindle it. Repeat the opening of your mind, your mental housecleaning and your anticipation. But do not assume that the Holy Spirit has not heard or answered. He has already answered. I think it is all right to repeat the question, as long as you do it in the spirit of clearing out your own cobwebs, rather than reminding a Holy Spirit that you think has nodded off.

Keep alert for the answer and you will know it when it comes.

The Holy Spirit does not forget your request. And if you do not forget, then chances are you will inwardly recognize the answer when it comes. In my experience, answers usually come accompanied by a little tag or bell in my mind that, in essence, says, "This is it." If that little bell goes off, trust it, even if at first you do not understand what the answer it pointed out means.

If in doubt about what you receive, apply the rules of discernment and/or seek confirmation.

Of course, many times we receive something and do not know if it is the real thing. At that point, you can seek guidance to confirm it, and/or you can use the rules of discernment, which we will be discussing in the next chapter.

CHAPTER 5

Discernment

The issue of discerning true guidance from false guidance, and discerning true from false within the same piece of guidance, is one of the biggest, hardest and stickiest issues in the whole arena of guidance. Yet it is an issue that absolutely has to be confronted. For this is one bull that, if you do not take it by the horns, is going to gore you. I will cover two forms of discernment: separating out the false elements in guidance that originates from the Spirit, and separating out inspired ideas from ideas that you invented.

Separating out false elements in real guidance

The usual image of guidance is what I call the Flaming Finger approach. If you have ever seen the movie, *The Ten Commandments*, you probably recall the scene on Mount Sinai in which God hovers in a cloud a little ways off from the side of the mountain. Then, as His low, booming voice utters each commandment, an arm of flame flies out of the cloud and smashes into the stone tablet, burning the commandment onto the tablet in fiery letters.

The idea that what makes it onto the tablet, or onto the page, or out of our lips, is straight from God is about as simplistic and naive as you could get. If you really work with guidance, either you are forced to just abandon the Flaming Finger perspective, or you end up doing a lot of rationalizing and convenient forgetting. For guidance is one of the more tricky things you will ever get your hands on. When it comes to you it seems so obviously authoritative. But then when all the events have played out and you look back at the original guidance, your head may start spinning. Was the guidance right? Was it wrong? Was it both? In some situations, if you are really honest with yourself, you may never know.

Let me give you some examples. One of the more vexing phenomena in guidance is what I have come to call *foreshadowings*. A foreshadowing is an instance in which seemingly authentic guidance shows up, often repeated in many forms over a short time, telling you of something about to develop, something to be moved into. So you get ready for it all to unfold, hopes running high, and it doesn't. You later realize that it was really a foreshadowing of a future unfoldment. In fact, I have more than once seen these foreshadowings come true years later *to the day* from when they first occurred. To make things doubly tricky, twice now I have experienced two foreshadowings of the same thing. One will occur and suck me into thinking it is all going to break loose, and of course it doesn't. And then years later a second installment will come in the form of a whole set of signs and guidance that is strikingly parallel to the first set. Since I knew the first one was a foreshadowing, I figured that this one was the real thing. Yet it too turned out to be a foreshadowing.

In fact, I am not really sure that the guidance, by the time it makes it to our conscious experience, really *remembers* if it is talking about now or about the future, if you understand my meaning. I think that obviously the Spirit knows. But by the time His message has trickled down through the various levels of our minds, it may have lost touch with whether it is a foreshadowing or a message that applies to right now. Luckily, however, even foreshadowings move us in what is ultimately the right direction. Yet I also think that if you are wise to them, you can save yourself a lot of false starts, as well as a lot of embarrassing announcements.

Even more baffling than foreshadowings are the following. I have now experienced two occasions—separated by several years—in which the same puzzling pattern showed up. In each case there was a group endeavor that had been going on for years and was now reaching a watershed point: Things would either go upward from here or would begin to disintegrate. At this point, two sets of signs came. Each set was integrated and unmistakably clear. One set said that things are about to repair themselves and begin climbing upward. The other set said the exact opposite, that they were poised on the brink of disintegration. This crazy situation was finally resolved as one of the sets completely unravelled over time. None of its signs came to fruition; they all crashed and burned. Eventually the other set proved totally correct and true. Now, my experience has been that if I receive a clear set of signs, it is very trustable. Yet here were two instances in which a whole set proved not only incorrect, but precisely opposite to the truth. I have ideas about why such a thing may happen, but to be perfectly honest, I still do not understand it.

Another example comes from Helen Schucman's scribing of the Course. I love reading in *Absence from Felicity* about the early

Course scribing, for Helen's mind would distort the guidance from Jesus, and he would then come back and tell her what her mind did and give her the corrected version. My favorite instance was where she receives a miracle principle which says, "Miracles are cobwebs of iron. They unite human frailty [symbolized by the cobwebs] with the strength of God [symbolized by the iron]" (*Absence from Felicity*, p. 227)—an interesting thought and colorfully presented. Yet later, Jesus comes back to her and tells her, if I understand his point, that iron is a better symbol for the seeming strength of the human body, which, like iron, is crude and heavy. And that cobwebs represent how airy and ephemeral the body really is, thus indicating that our strength cannot come from it but must come from elsewhere, from God. He then goes on: "The point should read 'A miracle reawakens the awareness that the spirit, not the body, is the altar of Truth...'" (*Absence from Felicity*, p. 228). Now, the implication here is that this is what he originally told her and that it was her mind that invented the whole cobweb and iron thing; that her mind distorted a point about abandoning the body as a source of strength and turning to the true source, the spirit, into a point about taking our weakness and merging it with the strength of spirit.

This kind of thing, in which our minds take a true impulse from the Spirit and falsely translate it, is perhaps the rule, rather than the exception, in receiving guidance. A couple years ago, a friend of mine received very powerful and authoritative inner guidance to solve her family's financial problems by sending out a chain letter. At the time she was unaware of the fact that chain letters are not only illegal, but arguably unethical, in that they simply redistribute money from the many to the few. So she abandoned the idea and chalked it up to false guidance. Then, over a period of months, many forms and instances of guidance came that clarified the matter. Eventually it seemed clear that the Spirit was trying to communicate to her that their financial problems would be helped by distributing spiritual publications through the mail. And that, apparently, the chain letter guidance was her mind's mistranslation of this impulse, a mistranslation that was made possible by her conscious ignorance about chain letters. At least that is our best guess at this time; we feel the situation is still evolving.

If we understood the human mind, this would all seem natural. For it is not the case that there is just our conscious mind, and then, right on the other side of it, the cloud of God's Presence, complete with Flaming Finger. I once heard a Sufi say that between our conscious minds and God are 70,000 veils. True guidance, then, has to travel through all of those veils. Perhaps a better analogy is 70,000 panes of smoky, distorted glass; smoky, because each pane is at least slightly tinted by ego; distorted because each pane is mental, intelligent, and so is intelligently curved so as to distort in a particular way the light passing through it. Because of this, what starts out as a message about the altar of truth, once it passes through those 70,000 panes, comes out talking about cobwebs and iron; or a message about mailing spiritual publications comes out saying "send a chain letter;" or, who knows, a message about strengthening your faith comes out saying, "Kill the heathens;" or a message about ego surrender comes out calling for animal sacrifice.

And this, of course, is why everyone gets different guidance. If you think, for instance, that if you put a collection of people who receive inner guidance in the same room and ask them the same questions, that they would all come up with the same answers—or even compatible answers—then you are in for a surprise. This is also why Helen Schucman speaks to Jesus and receives a psycho-spiritual system smacking heavily of Eastern non-dualism, while visionaries speak to Jesus' mother for the last 150 years and receive pure Catholicism, so pure that I doubt you could remain even a Protestant and completely believe it.

What do we do with this fact of mistranslation, with the human mind's refraction of guidance; especially since, as I said, I think this is really the rule, rather than the exception? There are several things that I have found helpful in dealing with this ever-present phenomenon.

Trust the kernel, but be open about the shell.

When you receive guidance, one way to look at it is that it has both an outer shell and an inner kernel. Your task is to mentally separate the two and to carry completely different attitudes toward them. With the shell, be extremely open. Realize that it may end up being just plain wrong, or partially wrong, or who knows what. The more specific it gets, the less attached to its form you should become. Yet, if the guidance really has a ring to it, trust the kernel. Realize it is a real impulse from the Spirit, a real ray of light into this murky dream world, a genuine hand from above lowered down to lift you up.

Of course, knowing what exactly the kernel is can be pretty problematic. With the above examples of Helen's cobwebs of iron guidance and my friend's chain letter guidance, there was no way to identify what the kernel was at first. Only subsequent guidance revealed it. Further, the kernel may not be one thing; it may be in layers. In fact, a more accurate metaphor may be that of an onion, in which there are several concentric rings, each inner ring being a sort of kernel in relation to the rings outside of it. When you receive a particular piece of guidance, then, you may be getting an onion in which all the rings are true, in which only some of them are true, or in which only the innermost ring is true. How can you know?

I think that, in many instances, when you have just received the guidance, you cannot. There is no way to know. So what do you do? The following are some suggestions:

Follow the shell with an open, provisional, experimental attitude.

It is as if you have been given a path to walk to a certain destination. You care only about reaching the destination, not about the particular path. And you have no way of knowing if this path really will get you to your goal. So start on it, but stay alert, have no attachment to it, and be ready to branch off onto another path at a moment's notice.

Run on new guidance.

Because those shells are so often unreliable, the further you get away from them in time, the more unreliable they get. Just like your body runs best on fresh food, so your life runs best on fresh guidance.

Do not be afraid to make a mistake.

Remember, it is not how pretty the process looks, it is whether or not you make it to the destination. And making it to the destination is a function of how much you want to, not how antiseptic your process has been. As God's child, you have been given a universe of room in which to make mistakes. If your heart is true, truth will find its way to you even in the midst of your craziest mistakes.

Trust repeating themes.

My favorite technique is to only get very sure once I have had a particular theme show up in many instances of guidance. Being generally terrified of mistakes, I have found this method to be very safe. In other words, if you get a lot of onions thrown at you, and despite their different outer rings they all have the same collection of inner rings, then it is safe to assume that those inner rings are from the Holy Spirit.

Realizing the difference between the shell and the kernel,

and realizing its underlying basis—the difference between our separated mind and the Holy Spirit's Mind—I think it is useful to carry a two-fold mental posture when it comes to the degree of certainty we carry about our direction:

Absolute conviction about what has been given by the Spirit.

When we are really sure that something has come from the Holy Spirit, and we have reliably identified the kernel of it as opposed to the shell, we should have faith in it. We should see it as a lifeline that we can hang onto regardless of the appearances swirling around us. Time and time again I have seen seemingly immovable appearances give way in favor of apparently impossible guidance. In the end, real guidance is more real than even the most solid of appearances in this shadow world. If you are holding real guidance in your hand, trust it with your life.

Absolute openness about what has not been given by the Holy Spirit.

It is valuable to have great appreciation not only for the fact that apart from the Holy Spirit we do not know, but also for the fact that it can be very difficult to tell when He has really spoken. So where we are not yet certain that He has, we must have a mind as open as the sky. We must have great tolerance for uncertainty, ambiguity, loose ends, messy pictures. We must be all right with confusion and paradox, multiple possibilities and the ever-impending likelihood of instant change and mental reorientation. A mind that needs to have every puzzle solved and every bit of data packed away in neat mental boxes is going to have trouble, I feel, being authentically guided.

Obviously, maintaining both of these postures can be very challenging, for they tend to tear each other down. The temptation is to use mental openness to tear down and mistrust true guidance, or to use true guidance to map everything out in order to soothe your mind's need for certainty. The trick is to stand on the ground of genuine guidance alone; to stand your ground, but only your ground. It is all right to use your power of reasoning to generalize from this ground outward, but do so experimentally and tentatively. And even while you are standing your ground on faith, be open about that ground. Realize that you may have falsely concretized a true impulse from the Spirit. Yet, on the other hand, even while you are uncertain, do not be afraid to experiment and to step out boldly, knowing that if your willingness is equally bold, all mistakes can be corrected.

Discerning your ideas from the Spirit's ideas

In addition to mistranslations, there are instances in which what masquerades as guidance is just pure ego. I think that purely egoic guidance can come through such apparently inspired means as inner voice, but most often it comes from ideas that pop into our minds or from significance we inappropriately read into dreams or outer events. Wherever it comes from, I have found that the temptation to think a completely ego-laden idea is truly guided is very great and hence very common. I think a good amount of the ideas that we think are really hot, and even definitely inspired, are simply what our egos want us to believe.

So, how do we separate out the true from the false? Perhaps the main quality that can help us here is real, unflinching self-honesty. We must have the ability to put things on the table and objectively examine them. We must care more about truth than about our own desires. I find that this issue of self-honesty is central in most attempts to discern. What I mean is that the answer to whether a piece of guidance is true or false is usually somewhere in, or not far from, our conscious minds, and we simply do not want to look at what we already know. All of us have fears and attachments. The trick is not to not have them. It is to treat them dispassionately as objective factors, to throw them out on the table alongside everything else and look at them, almost as if they were someone else's fears and attachments.

So, in any attempt to discern whether an idea is guided or not, ask yourself what you would conclude if you had the courage to admit to yourself what you really already know. This is the heart of discernment. To help you better tune into what you already know, the following are two sets of criteria I have found that more often than not hold true. I say "more often than not," because in the world of guidance, my experience is that nothing *always* holds true.

The marks of your own mind

I have found that the things that my mind conjures up have a distinctive feel to them and a distinctive set of qualities. The following "marks of your own mind" attempt to capture that. These, then, are indicators that the idea you have a hold of is of your own making, not the Holy Spirit's.

1. Part of a mental train or mental skyscraper.

Each of us sees our lives in terms of a massive framework we have built in our minds. One way to think of this mental framework is as a giant skyscraper. The foundation of the building symbolizes the primary, essential goal we have chosen for our existence. We then mentally build on top of that. Each floor is a means for the goal beneath it as well as the goal of the means above it. In other words, as the floors go up, the original goal is increasingly specified, increasingly translated into specific means.

Now, most of our ideas about what to do are simply an example of our adding another floor to the top of this skyscraper. They arise because they seem to be the logical means for attaining the goals beneath them, which arose because they seemed to be means for the goals beneath them, etc., etc. These ideas feel right and exciting because they give us a shot of hope that our goals might be accomplished. They derive their power in us by virtue of their connection to the rest of the building.

The problem is that, if we are the ones who built the sky-scraper, its foundational goal is simply the reinforcement and preservation of our egos. And all the floors above that are just different shapes of attack. Standing at the top floor, which is teeming with its new ideas of how to make things work, it is nearly impossible to see that. But it is true nonetheless.

Another metaphor to use is that of a mental train composed of a series of cars. This metaphor is time-oriented, in that it represents our projection of goals into the future. The engine that pulls the whole thing is our major goal for our eventual future. What we generally do is work back from the engine. We generate goals and strategies starting with the more distant future and working backwards, getting closer and closer to the present, until we reach a course of action for the present moment. In other words, we add cars on and create a long train, all pulled by the engine. Most new ideas that we come up with, then, are just the last car on the train.

My point is this: If an idea you have is the last car on the train or the top floor of the skyscraper, you can feel it. You can sense the other cars or floors connected to the idea. You can feel the juice that it draws from that connection, the excitement, importance and "rightness" that it draws from its relationship with the other cars or floors. If you can feel this connection, chances are the idea is of your own making and not of the Holy Spirit.

2. Feels exciting, tempting.

Self-generated ideas, because of their connection to our ego's goals, often feel very exciting, exhilarating, even hypnotic. There is a certain intensity to which the mind clings to them, as if they must be true, as if they cannot be let go of, as if they need our attachment to hold them in place, being without foundation on their own, and as if we fear that the Spirit will come and take them away from us. I think that true guidance is often very exciting. But if the excitement has a feeling of intense attachment to a pleasure that must be defended, then chances are it is your idea, not the Spirit's. Like all these criteria, however, this one can be tricky. For we often have an inappropriate ego-attachment to an idea that is truly guided.

3. Feels wrong.

A self-generated idea will often feel two very different ways. While on the surface it may be exciting, if you quiet your mind and feel down as far as you can, you will find that below the excitement it feels completely different. On this deeper level it can feel one of many ways: dead, lifeless, heavy, strained, forced, conflicting, discordant, foul, stained, dirty, fishy, slimy. These feelings are extremely telling and deserve to be listened to and respected.

If we put points 2 and 3 together, we can see that a self-generated idea feels sort of like dessert: heavy, instantly pleasuring, but with no deeper satisfaction.

4. Pits the needs of one against the needs of others.

This one can be tricky, for true guidance does not always make everyone happy. Yet our own ideas are notorious for not respecting the needs of others and for elevating and glorifying our own position. I will say more about how to use this idea properly in the next set of criteria.

The marks of the Holy Spirit

Just as with the marks of your own mind, none of the following marks of the Spirit are absolute guidelines. Each one of them may steer you wrong at different times. Yet, as a whole, they paint a picture that is a different world than that painted by the marks of your own mind.

1. Feels right deep inside.

This one is perhaps the most important mark. When an idea comes, set aside your surface reactions and take a moment to really feel down inside of your mind, trying to reach the deepest place of which you are aware. If it is true guidance, chances are that in that place in you the idea will feel right. Just as with the wrongness we discussed a few points ago, this rightness may take many forms: a calm, solid certainty, a clarity of pure knowing, a rightness or trueness, a purity, a serene, rarified holiness, a high vibration, a holy glow. There is just a certain mental quality that goes along with true guidance. You could call it a mental odor of holiness, a perfume of the Spirit. And the more often you have smelled it, the more quickly and reliably you can identify it.

I feel it is important to trust your mind to smell this perfume, even if you have attachments and blocks, even if you are not able to smell it at first. Real guidance has a way of being recognized as clearly authentic even when feelings are running strongly the other way. I have seen countless situations in which people did not like what came through, yet at the same time sensed its authenticity so clearly that fighting it was out of the question. As we said in Chapter 2, trust implicitly your ability to follow, even if shadows surround it.

On the other hand, your internal sensors will probably only be reliable if the guidance is about an issue that is facing you right *now*. If it is facing someone else or is about a distant future, then my experience is that your best intuitions may be completely worthless. So do not view your internal sense as the All-Seeing Eye, but know that it will be there for you when you really need it.

2. Feels challenging.

This is not by any stretch always true, but it is very often true. And this is why I think that talking about true guidance as primarily marked by peace or bliss can be misleading. The peace that would most readily lead us is our ego's desire to sit fat and happy. Yet real guidance often directly frustrates the ego's desires and needs. And so while the guidance may have a peaceful feel to it deep down, it may cause us to consciously feel very challenged.

Putting together the above two marks of the Spirit with two of the marks of our own minds, we can see that quite often our ideas feel exciting but wrong, whereas the Spirit's ideas often feel challenging but right. You might ask yourself, "Does this feel more like a hot fudge sundae or an angelic choir?" My favorite way to encapsulate this dichotomy is a story from the famous fantasy trilogy, *The Lord of the Rings*, by J.R.R. Tolkien. In it, the hobbits meet up with a suspicious-looking man of the wilderness named Strider. He offers to help them, but the hobbits do not know if they should trust him. They fear he could be a servant of the Enemy. Finally, they decide that a servant of the Enemy would *look fair* but *feel foul*, whereas Strider, on the other hand, *looks foul* but *feels fair*. And, as it turns out, he is actually the true King, who is just looking very worn from his long travels.

3. Is surprising, fresh, unthought of.

Real guidance is not always surprising, but frequently it is. In fact, the quality of freshness and surprise is one of the surest marks of real guidance, for it comes to you from outside of your whole mental framework. It is coming from a Mind that may be within your mind, yet is still outside your conscious faculties. Thus, it will often seem like it has come out of the blue, like it is an idea that has no history or past. It will feel like a fresh approach, something that your mind has cleanly missed yet which is still the perfect solution.

4. Reframes things.

The Holy Spirit has a whole different way of thinking than you do. In fact, He has built His own skyscraper, which is a completely different building than yours. The foundation of His skyscraper is not ego preservation, but ego relinquishment. He has brought that goal up floor by floor, translating it into increasingly specific means of attainment. Finally, He has built the top floor, which is His guidance for you in this situation at this moment. It is what you can do right at this moment to serve the ultimate goal of total ego relinquishment.

And just as your own ideas clearly imply the rest of your mental skyscraper, His ideas clearly imply His skyscraper. And because His building is a radically different animal than yours, His answer is going to reframe things. It is going to replace, at least in part, your mental framework with His, your perspective, your way of thinking, with His. This is why, as I said earlier, one of the most frequent and vexing habits of true guidance is to not quite answer your question as you framed it and instead imply that your question was an expression of the problem rather than a pure seeking of the answer.

5. Satisfies everyone's true needs at once.

This is one of the real marks of the Spirit. One of this world's great illusions is that my needs are in conflict with yours. From this idea are born all the ills of the world. Yet the Course tells us that, since in truth we are the same Self, it is impossible for our interests to be in conflict. Somehow, we are simply not allowed into situations in which a real conflict of needs can arise. And thus, as my needs and your needs become unable to be met by the same thing, we automatically find ourselves leaving each other's physical presence and going our apparently separate ways.

Authentic guidance has a way of reflecting the fact that our interests cannot really be in conflict. A situation can seem impossible. It can seem as if you simply have to choose whose needs to meet and whose needs to trash. This, however, is because we do not see deeply enough into the situation. If we did we would see a much larger range of alternatives. One of the things I have learned is that the Spirit *always* sees more alternatives than you do. Never assume that you see all the alternatives. The alternatives you see are based on your skyscraper, not His, and reflect the limitations of your thinking. When real guidance comes it will often amaze you with its ability to thread 2 or 5 or 50 needles at once.

Sometimes the fact that a piece of guidance is meeting everyone's true needs at the same time is quite apparent. The truth of it hits you at once. Yet sometimes it seems as if what turns out to be authentic guidance has frustrated the needs of one or more of the people involved. I think this arises because we are often totally out of touch with our true needs. We think our needs are for the gratification of our egos, while our true needs are for waking up from the ego. Thus, I think that the more in touch we are with our real need to heal and awaken, the more we will see the perfect appropriateness of real guidance when it comes.

Go back to its genesis

One final important tool of discernment is to go back to the moment when an idea was born. Oftentimes the moment of birth is the moment of truth. Whether an idea is a human invention or a spiritual inspiration will frequently be evident in its genesis. So, when you are in doubt about the source of an idea, go back to that genesis and ask yourself these questions:

Did it arrive in an inspired, spontaneous way?

When it first came, before your mind got to work on it, did it have a ring of truth, was there a clear knowing in you? I find that when an inspired idea comes into my mind, there is often a distinctive feel to it that identifies it as inspired. It is almost like a bell is rung in my mind, or there is a feeling that this idea was placed in me from above.

Did it arrive in a calculated way,

as an expression of resentment, as a vehicle for your specialness? What precise motive gave it birth? As you trace back in your mind, if you notice that the idea was born out of a motive to satisfy some ego desire, grudge or agenda, then you can be fairly sure that it is not from the Spirit and will not serve His plan.

Overall, then, we can say this about discerning true from false guidance: If an idea comes to you that is born out of your desire to satisfy your goals and agendas; if it fits those goals and agendas to a tee and therefore expresses your belief that your needs are in conflict with the needs of others; if it feels exciting on the surface due to its promise to satisfy your goals, but underneath that it feels dead and forced; then set it aside and heave a sigh of relief. Yet if it comes with an inspired ring to it; if it is an unexpected surprise, a fresh idea that reframes things and suggests a different way of thinking, a different set of goals; if, however challenging it seems, it feels truly right and appears to meet everyone's healthy needs; then chances are it is from the Spirit.

CHAPTER 6

Guidance as a
Way of Life

As I said in the Introduction, I fully believe that guidance can form the basis for a new way of moving through life. I also believe that when the time is right it can form much of the basis for a new world, including a new way of doing business and a new form of government. For guidance, in my experience, is a very real and available phenomenon, which, with learning and experience, can reliably be used to govern all the affairs that used to be governed by our walled-off, adversarial, ego-ridden minds. When the Spirit is really invited in as the Guiding Force in a situation, something truly different happens. Whole new possibilities are opened up. Things that seemed impossible come to pass. People mature beyond anyone's expectations. Different positions, rather than polarizing, find common ground. Connections—mental, physical and interpersonal—are made that could never have been anticipated. Creative talents are discovered and find expression. Fresh approaches and solutions come into being. The whole limiting framework of human life and society is slowly transcended as one by one gaps are bridged and walls are jumped. And all of it seems to bubble up from some spiritual Ground that is almost motherly in Its providential care.

This is the guided life in its maturity. Yet most of us are a long way from this kind of life. All we can do is put our first foot down and begin the journey of a thousand miles. How can we do that? How can we either take our first step towards a more guided life or perhaps take our next step on a journey that we have already consciously begun?

I think one good beginning point is to conduct a guidance experiment. Take some relevant issue in your life and really seek an answer about it. Use whatever tools you have found in this booklet and elsewhere to elicit guidance from the Spirit. And do it not just to find healing in this one area of your life. Do it as an experiment, a pilot project, which, if successful, will be the beginning of a new way of life.

Another good step is to sit down and either in your mind or on paper have a long conversation with the Holy Spirit. Tell Him that you really want to live by His guidance. Tell Him about all your desires to do this. Open up to Him all the blocks you have to doing this and explore them with Him. Be perfectly open and honest, both in your attraction to and recoil from being guided. If you really mean business, something will soon come into your life that will help you. There is no way to predict its form, but stay alert and watch for it and you will know it when it comes.

Whatever you choose to do, I hope this booklet will in some way have served to move you closer to a guided way of life, to relinquishing your control and turning it over to a Presence Who yearns to shepherd you through all the storms of this world and bring you safely home.

the **Circle** of **A**tonement

Teaching & Healing Center

·*Publications*·

·*Products*·

·*Services*·

based on **A Course in Miracles**

The Circle of Atonement
Teaching and Healing Center

is a non-profit, tax-exempt corporation founded in 1993, and is located in Sedona, Arizona. It is based on *A Course in Miracles*, the three-volume modern spiritual classic, which we believe was authored by Jesus through a human scribe.

A Note from the President

Dear Student:

Our conviction at The Circle of Atonement is that *A Course in Miracles* is a gold mine of spiritual wisdom, to be mined with the greatest care and respect. As we have attempted to do this, we believe we have found an answer to the perennial question of Course students, "How do I make it practical?" Our discovery is that the Course makes itself practical; that *A Course in Miracles* is a spiritual program laid out in detail, designed to lead us step-by-step to the lofty heights of which it speaks. If we simply follow its instructions, we will become happier, more loving and forgiving people, well on our way to complete liberation.

Our materials at the Circle are meant to help the student do just that: take the Course as a program. They are designed to aid the student in the study of the Text, the practice of the Workbook, and the fulfillment of one's function as a teacher of God. We offer these materials to you in the hope that they can serve you well on your journey home.

In Peace,

Robert Perry

P.S. We are committed to making our materials available to anyone regardless of their ability to pay. Please see our financial policy.

Mission Statement

> To discern the author's vision of *A Course in Miracles* and manifest
> that in our lives, in the lives of students, and in the world.

1

To faithfully discern the author's vision of *A Course in Miracles.*

In interpreting the Course we strive for total fidelity to its words and the meanings they express. We thereby seek to discover the Course as the author saw it.

To be an instrument in Jesus' plan to manifest his vision of the Course in the lives of students and in the world.

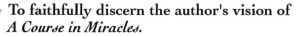

We consider this to be Jesus' organization and therefore we attempt to follow his guidance in all we do. Our goal is to help students understand, as well as discern for themselves, the Course's thought system as he intended, and use it as he meant it to be used – as a literal program in spiritual awakening. Through doing so we hope to help ground in the world the intended way of doing the Course, here at the beginning of its history.

3

To help spark an enduring tradition based entirely on students joining together in doing the Course as the author envisioned.

We have a vision of local Course support systems composed of teachers, students, healers, and groups, all there to support one another in making full use of the Course. These support systems, as they continue and multiply, will together comprise an enduring spiritual tradition, dedicated solely to doing the Course as the author intended. Our goal is to help spark this tradition, and to assist others in doing the same.

4

To become an embodiment, a birthplace of this enduring spiritual tradition.

To help spark this tradition we must first become a model for it ourselves. This requires that we at the Circle follow the Course as our individual path; that we ourselves learn forgiveness through its program. It requires that we join with each other in a group holy relationship dedicated to the common goal of awakening through the Course. It also requires that we cultivate a local support system here in Sedona, and that we have a facility where others could join with us in learning this approach to the Course. Through all of this we hope to become a seed for an ongoing spiritual tradition based on *A Course in Miracles.*

Friends of the Circle
JOINING IN A COMMON VISION

If the vision of the Circle presented here speaks to you, we invite you to join with us in it. Ask yourself: Is this a vision I want to see promulgated in the world? Is this something I want to give my support to? If so, perhaps you would like to become a "Friend of the Circle." The benefits include:

Category 1: $60.00 per year*

- Four-issue subscription to our newsletter, *A Better Way*
- *Friends Newsletters*, updates and special reports, making you an informed partner
- Support in your study and application of the Course
- Special materials and handouts
- Feedback forms to share with us your ideas and concerns
- Join us in our daily Workbook and meditation practice

Category 2: $130.00 per year* - Includes all of the above, plus

- Products and services, valued at a total of $70.00 (including appropriate shipping fees)

Quarterly payment plans are available for both categories, at a slightly higher cost.

*ALL PRICES ARE FOR U.S. ONLY, and are subject to change. Please contact The Circle of Atonement at (520) 282-0790 for the most current information.

TO BECOME A FRIEND OF THE CIRCLE

- Confirm the current price for the category membership you desire with the Circle.
- Write us a paragraph or two about why you want to become a Friend. What about this speaks to you?
- Take a few moments to silently join with us in purpose.
- Enclose your initial payment/donation (If you are unable to afford the amount listed, see our Financial Policy page 79).

Services Currently Offered

NEWSLETTER, BOOKS AND BOOKLETS - *A Better Way* is the Circle's newsletter, published quarterly. It is primarily a teaching journal, containing articles by Robert Perry, Allen Watson, Greg Mackie and others, on the Course.

Our other publications, ranging in size from booklets to full-size books, are available in bookstores or directly from The Circle of Atonement. They are expositions of a theme or section from the Course.

THE LEARNING CIRCLE - This is our school for students of the Course, and is a division of the Teaching Wing. It is designed to aid students in their reading, study and understanding of the Course. The school, started in 1994, consists of introductory classes and topical studies. Audio tapes with handouts are available following the completion of the classes in Sedona. Electronic Text Classes (ETC) are also offered. (See page 90.)

WORKSHOPS, SEMINARS AND RETREATS - The Circle currently offers workshops, seminars and retreats in Sedona. These are open to all individuals interested in *A Course in Miracles*. Dates and specifics are announced in every newsletter mailing (or call the Circle for more information and dates of events). Circle teachers, Robert Perry and Allen Watson, are available to speak at other locations by invitation.

"THIS ONE YEAR WE GIVE TO GOD" – For the year 2000 the Circle is conducting an intense program of study, practice and support here in Sedona. This program will carry us through the Workbook and the entire Text in one year. Each weekday morning we gather for ninety minutes to practice our Workbook lesson. Each weekday afternoon we study a Text section for another ninety minutes. This program is being taught by Robert, who is also available for one-to-one support. In addition, there is a rich environment of mutual support among the participants, and newer students are encouraged to select a personal teacher, or Course mentor, from among the more experienced students. See Issue #29 of *A Better Way* for more information.

FINANCIAL POLICY

Our financial policy is based on a line in *Psychotherapy*, a supplement to *A Course in Miracles*: "One rule should always be observed: No one should be turned away because he cannot pay." Therefore, if you would like any of our materials or services and cannot afford them, simply let us know, and give what you are able.

The Circle is supported entirely by your purchases and gifts. Therefore, we ask you to look within to see if you might be led to support the Circle's vision financially with a donation above the list price of materials. We encourage you to give, not in payment for goods received, but in support of our present and future outreach. Please note that only amounts given over the list price are considered tax-deductible.

Please see *A Better Way*, Issue #18 for a more detailed explanation.

Our Teachers

Robert Perry brings to *A Course in Miracles* many years of private study and public teaching. He began teaching at Miracle Distribution Center in 1986, and has since then taught throughout North America and around the world. His teaching grows out of his dedication to the Course as his own path and his desire to assist others on this path. Over the years he has become a respected voice in Course circles and has written for many Course newsletters and magazines. Robert is the founder of The Circle of Atonement and the author of numerous books and booklets based on the Course, including the popular *An Introduction to "A Course in Miracles."*

Allen Watson is well known around the world to *A Course in Miracles* students for his helpful and insightful daily commentaries on the Workbook lessons which are on the Internet, as well as in book form, titled *A Workbook Companion, Volumes I, II and III.* Allen's gifted and spirited writing and teaching help students to unlock the meaning of *A Course in Miracles* for themselves. Allen is teaching a weekly class that is designed to cover the entire *A Course In Miracles* Text, section by section. His Text commentaries and Study Guides are also available through the Internet and are being published in a book series entitled *Light on the Text.*

Books & Booklets

BASED ON *A COURSE IN MIRACLES*

An Introduction to *A Course in Miracles* – Perry; *A brief overview of the Course;* 44 pp.; **$2.95***

ACIM Interpretive Forum "Prosperity and *A Course in Miracles"* *With Position Papers by Allen Watson and Tony Ponticello, and Response Papers by several participants, this*

journal seeks to explore the Course's position on material abundance and divine supply; 47 pp.; **$5.00***

The Elder Brother: Jesus in *A Course in Miracles* – Perry; *Jesus – the most celebrated man in history. We have prayed to him, loved him, feared him. But have we really known him?*

Perry examines the historical Jesus and compares him with the author of the Course. Was the Course authored by Jesus? Perry offers his own opinion as he lets the reader come to his or her own conclusion. Fascinating and inspiring reading for anyone interested in Jesus or the Course; 184 pp.; **$9.00***

#1 Seeing the Face of Christ in All Our Brothers – Perry; *How we can see the Presence of God in others. This booklet seeks to present the Course's lofty vision of our Divine nature;* 47 pp.; **$5.00***

#3 Shrouded Vaults of the Mind – Perry; *Draws a map of the mind reflecting ACIM, and takes you on a tour through its many levels;* 44 pp.; **$5.00***

#4 Guidance: Living the Inspired Life Perry; *Drawn from ACIM and Perry's own experience, this booklet sketches an overall perspective on guidance and its place on the spiritual path;* 72 pp.; perfect bound; **$7.00***

#6 Reality & Illusion: An Overview of Course Metaphysics Part I – Perry; *Examines the Course's vision of reality, attempting to answer the question: "What is real?";* 44 pp.; **$5.00***

#7 Reality & Illusion: An Overview of Course Metaphysics Part II – Perry; *Examines questions such as: "Why are we here?" "How did we get here?" Discusses the origins of our apparent separation from God, and how to surmount the barriers to ultimate happiness;* 52 pp.; **$5.00***

#8 A Healed Mind Does Not Plan Watson; *Examines our approach to planning and decision-making, showing how it is possible to leave the direction of our lives up to the Holy Spirit;* 40 pp.; **$5.00***

#9 Through Fear to Love – Watson; *Explores two sections from ACIM that deal with our fear of redemption and with the perception of the world that results from our fearful self-perception. It leads the reader to see how we can look on ourselves with love;* 44 pp.; **$5.00***

#10 The Journey Home Watson; *Sets forth a sequential description of the spiritual journey as seen in the Course. This booklet presents a map of sorts to give us an idea of our spiritual destination and what we must go through to get there;* 64 pp.; **$5.00***

#11 Everything You Always Wanted to Know About JUDGMENT But Were Too Busy Doing It to Notice

Perry & Watson; *A survey of various teachings about judgment in ACIM: What is judgment, giving up judgment, right use of judgment, judgment of the Holy Spirit, the Last Judgment;* 59 pp.; **$5.00***

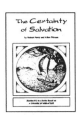

#12 The Certainty of Salvation – Perry & Watson; *An antidote to feelings of discouragement, impatience, despair and doubt that may arise for those trying to reach the spiritual goal of the curriculum of the Course. Gathers together many of the Course's most encouraging and uplifting thoughts, reassuring us that attaining the goal is inevitable;* 51 pp.; **$5.00***

#13 What Is Death?
Watson; *Our belief in death is at the core of our painful experiences in this world. The author presents philosophical*

insights from the Course about the nature of death, and seeks to explain how to apply these principles in practical situations such as the death of a loved one, or facing death ourselves; 42 pp.; **$5.00***

#14 The Workbook as a Spiritual Practice – Perry; *The Workbook of* A Course in Miracles *trains us in a profound new method of spiritual practice, and only through this practice will we realize the wonderful promises contained in the Course. This booklet is designed to help students get the most out of the Workbook, to help them find happiness through the training of their minds;* 57 pp.; **$5.00***

#15 I Need Do Nothing: Finding the Quiet Center
Watson; *This phrase captures the heart of the Course's philosophy, yet it has also been the source of endless misunderstanding. This paragraph-by-paragraph commentary on the section, "I Need Do Nothing," seeks to draw out that heart as well as clear up the misunderstandings;* 57 pp.; **$5.00***

#16 A Course Glossary
Perry; *The Course employs a unique use of language in which it fills familiar terms with new meaning. This makes its*

language initially confusing, yet eventually transformative. This glossary attempts to clear up the confusion. Along with Course meanings, definitions include root, conventional, and Christian meanings. Intended for both new and experienced students, both individual and group study; 96 pp.; perfect-bound; **$7.00***

#17 Seeing the Bible Differently: How *A Course in Miracles* Views the Bible
Watson; *Addresses the question, "How does the Course relate to the*

Bible?" Drawing on the Course's own attitude toward the Bible, it recognizes both similarities and differences, and emphasizes the continuity of God's message in the two books, seeing the Course as a clearer presentation of truth, which supersedes the Bible while standing clearly in its lineage; 80 pp.; perfect-bound; **$6.00***

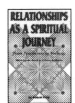

#18 Relationships as a Spiritual Journey: From Specialness to Holiness – Perry; *Describes the unique teaching of the Course on the subject of human relationships, that the quest for God is best accomplished in them. This requires, however, that our relationships go through profound transformation, from special relationships, based on the pursuit of individual specialness, to holy relationships, based on a truly common goal;* 192 pp.; perfect-bound; **$10.00***

A WORKBOOK COMPANION
Commentaries on the Workbook for Students from
A Course in Miracles
by Allen Watson and Robert Perry

A three-volume set designed to aid students of the Course in their practice and understanding of the Workbook's daily lessons. Each volume includes a commentary and a practice summary of each lesson, as well as periodic overviews of the training goals of various lessons. These are not a replacement of the lessons themselves, but are rather a companion, with explanations, personal anecdotes, and advice on how to carry out the lessons. Each volume is perfect-bound.

#19	**Volume I** – covers Lessons 1 - 120	(320 pp.)	**$16.00***
#20	**Volume II** – covers Lessons 121 - 243	(304 pp.)	**$16.00***
#21	**Volume III** – covers Lessons 244 - 365	(352 pp.)	**$18.00***

Special Offer **ALL THREE VOLUMES - $45.00** (Reg. $50.00)

#22 The Answer is a Miracle

Perry and Watson; A Course in Miracles *promises to teach its students miracles, and who would not want to learn that? Yet the Course redefines miracles, causing many students to simply be confused about them. This book attempts to clear up that confusion and place miracles back where they belong, at the center of the Course, where we can learn them.*; 112 pp.; perfect bound; **$7.00***

#23 Let Me Remember You: God in *A Course in Miracles*

Perry and Watson; *God is a central topic in human life and in A Course in Miracles. Little attention, however, has been given to God by most students and teachers of the Course. This book is an attempt to remedy that situation. It is designed to help readers gain, or perhaps, regain, a sense of God's relevance and immediacy.* 186 pp.; perfect bound; **$10.00***

#24 Bringing the Course to Life: How to Unlock the Meaning of *A Course in Miracles* for Yourself

Watson and Perry; *The words of A Course in Miracles, though beautiful and profound, are notoriously hard to understand. This book is designed to teach the student, through instruction, example, and exercises, how to read the Course. It is designed to transform the reading of the Course from a dry, frustrating experience into a living, personal encounter with truth;* 257 pp.; perfect-bound; **$12.00***

Source Material

FOR OUR PUBLICATIONS

The following four books are works that we encourage every student of the Course to own. By definition, a Course student owns the Course itself. But we also believe that the other three books below are highly valuable to one's journey with the Course. All of them contain additional material dictated by Jesus through Helen Schucman. For this reason, our writings draw on them frequently.

A Course in Miracles (Hardcover) **$29.95***

The Gifts of God

This volume primarily contains Helen Schucman's poetry, which Helen felt she "received" from a deeper place in her own mind, not from

the author of the Course. However, the volume closes with a fourteen-page piece, also called "The Gifts of God," which is not one of Helen's poems. Rather, it was perhaps Helen's final authentic scribing from Jesus. We, therefore, consider it part of the Course's "canon" and for that reason our publications sometimes quote from it. **$21.95***

Supplements to ACIM: Psychotherapy and Song of Prayer

These are two supplements to the Course, now together in one volume. They were dictated by the author of the Course to Helen

Schucman after the Course's completion. The Circle's publications refer to both supplements often, as they are the same teaching as the Course from the same author. **$9.95***

Absence from Felicity, by

Kenneth Wapnick. *This excellent "Story of Helen Schucman and Her Scribing of* A Course in Miracles*" has immense historical value for its telling of the story of the Course's birth. The reason that the Circle's writings often quote from it is that it also contains a great deal of personal guidance given by Jesus to Helen Schucman and Bill Thetford. It thus provides a window onto how Jesus envisioned the Course being applied in the everyday lives of two people.* **$16.00***

The Vision
of the Learning Circle

The Learning Circle is our school for students of *A Course in Miracles*. Our vision is to aid students in their personal study of the Course. Since the Course is a book, the foundational activity for any student is simply reading the book. This is doubly so for this particular course, for it makes the study and understanding of its thought system the foundation for walking its path. As the opening line of the Workbook says, "A theoretical foundation such as the text provides is necessary as a framework to make the exercises in this workbook meaningful."

Based on the above, that one reads the book, how one reads the book, and how much one understands its thought system are all crucial. All of these provide a foundation for giving meaning to the application of the Course. The purpose of The Learning Circle is to aid and support students in all of the above things:

~ *in reading the book*

~ *in reading it in a way that mines its treasures*

~ *in understanding what it says*

~ *in seeing how this understanding applies in our lives*

Our experience has been that this reading, study and understanding are indeed the foundation for the entire path of the Course. As students become more firmly grounded in this, their experience of the Course and their ability to apply it increase exponentially.

"Bill has very intelligently suggested that you both should set yourself the goal of really studying for this course. There can be no doubt of the wisdom of this decision, for any student who wants to pass it." (Message given to Helen Schucman, scribe of *A Course in Miracles*; found in *Absence from Felicity*, p. 285)

The Learning Circle

TAPE SETS

The unedited live classes given in Sedona for students participating in our school are available on audio tape.

101 Basic Introduction to
A Course in Miracles – Watson
Six 60-minute tapes $ 30.00
Familiarizes students with the perspective of the Circle's instructors; offers an overview of the Course's message and thought system; discusses the Course as a spiritual path; and more.

102 Bringing the Course to Life:
Turning Study Into Experience
Perry and Watson
Eight 90-minute tapes $ 40.00
An intensive focusing on methods and techniques for studying the Course, taking into consideration its unique presentation of its thought system. Includes a Study Guide. Provides the basis for the book of the same title.

Topical Study Series

Each tape set focuses on a particular theme derived from the Course, determined to be of interest or a keynote for understanding. Handouts are included with each tape set.

301 Perception and Vision
Perry
Ten 90-minute tapes $ 55.00
Includes: Projection makes perception; true perception and vision; dream roles and shadow figures; Holy Spirit's interpretation; eyes of the body and eyes of Christ.

302 The Holy Instant
Perry & Watson
Ten 90-minute tapes $ 55.00
Focuses on Chapter 15 of the Text and includes: What is a holy instant; entering and experiencing the holy instant; different kinds and uses of the holy instant.

303 Judgment
Perry & Watson
Ten 90-minute tapes $ 55.00
Includes: A study of what judgment really is; how the Holy Spirit uses judgment; how we can release it; and more.

304 The Certainty of Salvation
Perry & Watson
Ten 90-minute tapes $ 55.00
Includes: The what's, why's, and how's of salvation; our nature and the journey; God's changelessness; the happy learner; who walks with us?

305 We Are the Light of the World
Perry & Watson
Ten 90-minute tapes $55.00
An exploration of our function in this world as givers of forgiveness and healing. Includes: our special function, extension, our function is our happiness.

306 Holy Relationships
Perry & Watson
Ten 90-minute tapes $55.00
Covers this important and controversial topic in the Course, carefully defining what the Course means by holy relationships, how they begin, progress and reach their goal.

The Learning Circle ───────────

307 Forgiveness
Perry & Watson
Ten 90-minute tapes $55.00
The theory and practice of forgiveness; how the Course defines forgiveness contrasted with what the word means in our culture; forgiveness practices.

308 God
Perry & Watson
Ten 90-minute tapes $55.00
A comprehensive treatment of this central, but under-appreciated topic in the Course. What God is; our fear of God; what God knows about our earthly lives; God's relationship with the Holy Spirit; prayer.

309 A Course in *What?*
Perry & Watson
Ten 90-minute tapes $55.00
Topics include: What is a miracle? Are miracles internal or interpersonal? Do they heal bodies? What is a miracle worker? How is the Course a course *in* miracles?

310 Time
Perry & Watson
Ten 90-minute tapes $55.00
Includes: Eternity and the unreality of time; the ego's repetition of the past; entering the present moment; saving time; patience.

311 The Body
Perry & Watson
Ten 90-minute tapes $55.00
Everything about the body: pleasure, pain, appearance, attractiveness, sex, the senses, the body's neutrality, its origin, the Holy Spirit's use of the body.

312 The Holy Spirit at Work in Our Lives
Perry & Watson
Ten 90-minute tapes $55.00
Primarily focuses on the role of receiving guidance from the Holy Spirit, including how to hear Him, the daily practice of asking, resistance to hearing, discernment of what is heard.

313 Sickness and Healing
Perry & Watson
Ten 90-minute tapes $55.00
Why we get sick; how to view illnesses in ourselves and others; finding healing for ourselves; giving healing to others; our calling as healers of patients.

601 Psychotherapy: Purpose, Process and Practice
Perry
Eleven 90-minute tapes $60.00
An in-depth study of *Psychotherapy* ... which was dictated to Helen Schucman after the completion of the Course to provide guidance for therapists who want to practice therapy as an expression of the Course's principles. It also has applications for anyone who wants to be "truly helpful" to others.

---

*ALL PRICES ARE FOR U.S. ONLY,
and are subject to change.
Please contact the Circle directly
for the most current
information.

Manual Study Series

Study of the *Manual for Teachers*
Robert Perry

This class attempts to mine the rich teaching in the Manual for Teachers. In addition to the usual detailed paragraph-by-paragraph study of the specified sections, the class tries to discern and internalize the Manual's instructions to us as teachers of God (even though the term may only partially apply to us). As a manual for our own lives, what does it have to tell us about how to live our lives, walk our path, and carry out our function?

501: Introduction through Section 8	**$50.00**
502 : Sections 9 through 23	**$50.00**
503: Sections 24 through Epilogue	**$50.00**
Study Guides for each tape set	**$10.00**

Special Offer:
All 3 tape sets **$125.00** (Reg. $150)

The Learning Circle

W O R K S H O P & R E T R E A T T A P E S E T S

These tape sets are from one-day workshops and a one weekend retreat held in Sedona. All of the tape sets are unedited and include participants' comments and questions. In reproducing the tapes, we have tried to ensure good sound quality of both teachers and participants. Each tape set includes handouts.

9806 All Things Are Lessons God Would Have Me Learn
Perry & Watson, June 1998
Five 90-minute tapes $30.00

We have our usual way of talking about our life events as lessons, but what does the Course mean when it says these things are lessons, and how can we learn them?

9902 Who Are You?
Perry & Watson, February 1999
Three 90-minute tapes $20.00

The Course's view of who we are explodes every assumption we have about ourselves. We are not merely human beings who also happen to have a spark of divinity within us or a higher Self. What, then, are we, and how do we remember what we are?

9903 How Do We Find Inner Peace?
Perry, April 1999
One 90-minute tape $ 5.00

This talk explores the Course's unique perspective on what real peace is, and how we can find it.

9904 Metal Discs & Paper Strips: The Course on Money
Perry, April 1999
Four 90-minute tapes $25.00

Our fears and attachments around money imprison us. The Course teaches that we can see money differently so that we use it rather than allowing it to use us. We can approach it in a pure and holy way, a way that will bring us real peace.

WORKSHOP & RETREAT TAPE SETS

9906 I Am Here Only to Be Truly Helpful: Practices from the Text
Perry, June 1999
Four 90-minute tapes $25.00

The Workbook is known for its practical exercises, but the Text contains practices as well. This workshop focuses on understanding and using Text practices dealing with such topics as fear, anger, or interpersonal conflict, and incorporating them into our personal "problem-solving repertoire."

9909 Forgiveness: The Pathway Home
Perry & Watson, September 1999
Nine 60-minute tapes $55.00

The goal of this weekend retreat was to guide participants through a process of forgiving a particular person in their lives, using both theory and experiential exercises. The process is designed to take us from uncovering our resentment and guilt to seeing the other person as our holy savior. A **Forgiveness Notebook** containing handouts from the retreat is included.

SG9909 Forgiveness Notebook
alone   **$10.00**

> *Forgiveness is the only gift I give,*
> *because it is the only gift I want.*
> *And everything I give I give myself.*
> *This is salvation's simple formula.*
>   *(Workbook Lesson 297)*

9911 How to Meditate and Pray
Perry, November 1999
Four 90-minute tapes $25.00

Meditation and prayer are perhaps the supreme spiritual practices the world over. The Course utilizes them also, providing extensive teaching in its own methods of meditation and prayer. This workshop is designed to teach these methods which can immensely enrich our lives and empower us to change our perceptions of the world.

2001 How to Find Your Special Function, Perry, January 2000
Seven 90-minute tapes $45.00

We all have a basic need to be of use and to make a contribution within a larger whole. According to the Course, as we ascend the ladder of development, each of us will discover and take up a special role in the salvation of the world. This weekend workshop is designed to help you uncover, prepare for, and carry out the part you were born to play in God's plan.

2005 The Ladder of Prayer, Perry, May 2000
Seven 90-minute tapes $45.00

The Song of Prayer, dictated to Helen Schucman after the completion of *A Course in Miracles,* is a favorite among Course students. This workshop explores what *The Song of Prayer* says about prayer, forgiveness and healing, and how to incorporate its message into our lives.

Electronic Text Class

The Electronic Text Class (ETC) is an E-mail series of combined commentaries and study guides on the Text of *A Course in Miracles,* written by Allen Watson. Allen's Internet Workbook commentaries have generated such enthusiastic feedback that we decided to do something similar for the Text. These commentaries provide a bridge into the world of the Text. They help you to understand its message, appreciate its wonders, and see its relevance to your life; and they provide study tools to help you understand the Course on your own. They are designed for use by groups as well as individuals.

ETC Commentary Schedule & Format:

The Text commentaries are E-mailed weekly, with three 12 to 13-week trimesters every year. The expected duration of the on-line series is seven years. The commentaries are being published in a book series entitled *Light on the Text.*

Each commentary covers one section of the Text, and includes the following features:

• informal commentary for each paragraph of the Text
• study question(s) for each paragraph (with Answer Key)
• study notes
• suggested exercises

For a sample copy of an ETC, please e-mail us at the address below. For more information and assistance in subscribing on-line, please direct your web browser to:

nen.sedona.net/circleofa/news–etc.html

Subscription Cost:

1999 first trimester (6 wks) back issues	$10.00
1999 full year back issues	$42.00
Single trimester	$20.00
One year consisting of 3 consecutive trimesters	$50.00

How to Subscribe:

Fill out the catalog order form and mail it with your check or money order (U.S. funds only) or credit card information. You can also order by E-mail (using credit card *only*). Subscription E-mail should be sent to: info@circleofa.com.

Please be sure to clearly print your E-mail address and your regular mailing address on your subscription request.

A Better Way

The title of our Newsletter comes from Bill Thetford's comment to Helen Schucman that "There must be another way." (Quoted in *Absence from Felicity*, p. 93; see page 84 of this catalog.); and from Jesus' comment in the Course that, "Everyone eventually begins to recognize, however dimly, that there *must* be a better way" (T-2.III.3:6).

We hope that these newsletters will be helpful to you on your journey to this "better way."

A Better Way is designed as a teaching journal for students of the Course. *For subscription information, see page 94.*

Back issues of *A Better Way* newsletter are available for $2.00 per copy and Special Christmas Letter for $.50 each.

A Better Way

A Better Way

Issue #19   July 1997
*Who Wrote A Course in Miracles?
Part II*

- 12 Remedies for the Wandering
  Mind
- Bringing the Course to Life, Part 1,
  Allen Watson

Issue #20   Nov. 1997
*"Be In My Mind, My Father": An
Appreciation of the Prayer for
Lesson 232*

- Bringing the Course to Life, Part 2,
  Allen Watson
- Welcome Me Not Into a Manger
  (Christmas Message)
- Seeing the Meaning in the Idea
  for the Day
- Tips on Practice: Reading Aloud
  and Expanded Prayers, *Allen Watson*
- Tips for Study Groups: Using the
  Text Studies Tapes, *Allen Watson*
- Psychotherapy and *A Course in
  Miracles*, *Thomas Dunn*

Issue #21   Feb. 1998
Does God Know We Are Here?

- Bringing the Course to Life, Part 3,
  Allen Watson
- Being Truly Helpful
- Frequently Asked Questions: How
  can we distinguish between the ego
  and the Holy Spirit?, *Allen Watson*
- True Prayer

Issue #22   May 1998
The Course on Childhood

- Class 102, Bringing the Course
  to Life
- Bringing the Course to Life, Part 4,
  Allen Watson
- Misunderstood Passages: Trust
  Not Your Good Intentions,
  Allen Watson
- How Holy is the Smallest Grain
  of Sand!
- Let Me Behold My Savior

Issue #23   Aug. 1998
Course-Based Parenting, Part I

- Bringing the Course to Life, Part 5,
  Allen Watson
- Hearing God's Voice Means Joining,
  Allen Watson
- All My Sorrows End in Your
  Embrace
- A Self-Study Course?

Issue #24   Dec. 1998
How Do We Forgive?

- Bringing the Course to Life, Part 6,
  Allen Watson
- Course-Based Parenting, Part II
- Difficult Passages: Think Not You
  Made the World?
- The Birth of Holiness into this World
  (Christmas Message)

Issue #25   March 1999
This Is As Every Day Should Be

- Does Behavior Matter?, *Greg Mackie*
- Bringing the Course to Life, Part 7,
  Allen Watson

Issue #26   May 1999
*If A Brother Asks You For Something
Outrageous*

- Gentle Firmness, *Greg Mackie*
- Bringing the Course to Life, Part 8,
  Allen Watson
- Big Daddy or Divine Desert?

Issue #27   Aug. 1999
What is "A Course in Miracles?"

- Appreciating the Masterpiece, Pt. 1,
  Greg Mackie
- Artistic Techniques Used in the
  Course, *Greg Mackie*

A Better Way

A list of *Reprinted Articles* by Allen Watson and Robert Perry from other Course-based publications is available upon request. Please mark your interest on the Request Form.

A Better Way Subscription
4 Issues per Year

United States: $10.00

Canada & Mexico: ....$14.00 U.S. dollars

All Other Countries: ....$18.00 U.S. dollars

Information Request Form ──────

All publications and products listed previously are available as of this printing. ALL PRICES ARE IN U.S. DOLLARS, and are subject to change. In addition, new titles become available regularly; therefore, please contact the Circle directly for the most current information.

Information is available by writing or calling us at:

The Circle of Atonement
Teaching and Healing Center

P.O. Box 4238 • W. Sedona, AZ 86340
Phone: (520) 282-0790 • Fax: (520) 282-0523
In the U.S. toll-free: (888) 357-7520 (for orders only)
e-mail: info@circleofa.com
Or
You can learn more and order materials directly from our website at
http://nen.sedona.net/circleofa/
Or
You can send the form below to the above address
with your information:

- -

NAME ────────────────────────────

ADDRESS ──────────────────────────

CITY ──────────── PROVINCE/STATE ──────

COUNTRY ──────── POSTAL/ZIP CODE ──────

PHONE ────────────────────────────

❏ Please send me a packet including information on current products, newsletter subscriptions, The Learning Circle Program, Friends of the Circle membership and the Electronic Text Class.

❏ Please send me a free list of reprinted articles

GUID 8/00